AF225975

The Inner Story of the
New International Version

The Inner Story of the
New International Version

Reflections of an Original NIV Translator

MURRAY J. HARRIS

WIPF & STOCK · Eugene, Oregon

THE INNER STORY OF THE NEW INTERNATIONAL VERSION
Reflections of an Original NIV Translator

Wipf & Stock
An Imprint of Wipf and Stock Publishers
199 W. 8th Ave., Suite 3
Eugene, OR 97401

www.wipfandstock.com

PAPERBACK ISBN: 978-1-6667-8784-9
HARDCOVER ISBN: 978-1-6667-8785-6
EBOOK ISBN: 978-1-6667-8786-3

09/26/23

To Lynette,
my new
"fellow slave in the Lord"
(Col 4:7)

Contents

Illustrations

Preface

GIVEN THE FACT THAT the majority of the original New International Version (NIV) translators are no longer with us and have passed into the Lord's presence, I thought it would not be inappropriate for one of those original translators, now an octogenarian, to share some of his treasured memories about the making of this remarkable version. After all, no English translation of the Bible had eclipsed the King James Version (KJV, or Authorised Version) as the most widely read version of the Bible until the mid-1980s, when the NIV broke that record that had stood for some three hundred and seventy-five years.

Initial translation work began on the NIV as early as the late 1960s. In 1970, along with two separate colleagues at Trinity Evangelical Divinity School, I was invited to submit a preliminary translation of Colossians and Ephesians for submission to the Committee on Bible Translation (CBT), the committee tasked with producing the NIV. Then from 1984 to 1996 I was privileged to serve on that CBT until my return to New Zealand in retirement. (Further details are given in ch. 2).

Hopefully, you the reader will not be preoccupied simply with discovering my opinion about "gender-neutral" translations but will be eager to get a "behind-the-scenes" insight into the task of working on a translation project with its unparalleled demands and pleasures. Then this may stimulate a fresh appreciation for the myriad of scholars who, down through the centuries, have provided us in our own language with the treasures enshrined in Holy Scripture.

But there is also a subsidiary aim in writing this book—to celebrate and encourage the tendency of some English translations regularly to translate the Greek word *doulos* by its normal meaning, "slave." This explains the final two chapters.

Unless indicated, all translations of biblical verses or passages are mine.

Acknowledgments

Permission has been kindly given by Biblica, the International Bible Society, to reproduce information and photos relevant to the production of the NIV.

Various publishers have given permission to reproduce, usually with changes, material that first appeared in various books I authored: volumes 1 and 2 of *Navigating Tough Texts: A Guide to Problem Passages in the New Testament* (Bellingham, WA: Lexham, 2020, 2023); *Slave of Christ: A New Testament Metaphor for Total Devotion to Christ* (Downers Grove, IL: InterVarsity, 1999); *Jesus as God: The New Testament Use of* Theos *in Reference to Jesus* (Grand Rapids: Baker, 1992; Eugene, OR: Wipf and Stock, 2008); *Prepositions and Theology in the Greek New Testament* (Grand Rapids: Zondervan, 2012); *The Second Epistle to the Corinthians: A Commentary on the Greek Text* (Grand Rapids: Eerdmans, 2005); an article I authored in *Voices* magazine; an article in *The New Zealand Herald*; and a review in *The Churchman*.

Once again, I am indebted to two treasured friends of seventy-five years who have kindly read and helpfully commented on my manuscript—David Burt and Dr. Graham D. Smith.

Also, I gratefully acknowledge the skillful and patient editorial work at Wipf and Stock of Matthew Wimer, Emily Callihan, Dr. Rebecca Abbott, and Dr. Savanah Landerholm in preparing this book for publication.

Abbreviations

ASV	American Standard Version (1901)
Barclay	W. Barclay, *The New Testament*. Vol. 1: *The Gospels and the Acts of the Apostles* (1968); Vol. 2: *The Letters and the Revelation* (1969)
BBE	Bible in Basic English (NT, 1941; OT, 1949)
BDAG	*A Greek-English Lexicon of the New Testament and Other Early Christian Literature* (revised and edited by F. W. Danker; Chicago: University of Chicago, 2000), based on W. Bauer's *Griechisch-deutsches Wörterbuch* (6th ed.) and on previous English eds. by W. F. Arndt, F. W. Gingrich, and F. W. Danker
	References are given by page number and by a–d (= the four sections of the page)
Bruce, *Paraphrase*	F. F. Bruce, *An Expanded Paraphrase of the Epistles of Paul* (Exeter, UK: Paternoster, 1981)
Cassirer	H. W. Cassirer, *God's New Covenant: A New Testament Translation* (Grand Rapids: Eerdmans, 1989)
CEB	Common English Bible (2011)
CEV	Contemporary English Version (1995)
cf.	*confer* (Latin), compare

CSB	Christian Standard Bible (2017)
ed(s).	editor(s), edition(s)
ESV	English Standard Version (2001)
EVV	English versions of the New Testament or Bible
GNB	Good News Bible (1976)
GNT	Good News Translation (1992)
Goodspeed	E. J. Goodspeed, *The New Testament: An American Translation* (Chicago: University of Chicago Press, 1923)
Harris, *2 Cor*	M. J. Harris, *The Second Epistle to the Corinthians: A Commentary on the Greek Text*, edited by I. H. Marshall and D. A. Hagner (Grand Rapids: Eerdmans, 2005)
Harris, *Jesus*	M. J. Harris, *Jesus as God: The New Testament Use of* Theos *in Reference to Jesus* (Grand Rapids: Baker, 1992; reprint, Eugene, OR: Wipf & Stock, 2008)
Harris, *Prepositions*	M. J. Harris, *Prepositions and Theology in the Greek New Testament* (Grand Rapids: Zondervan, 2012)
Harris, *Slave*	M. J. Harris, *Slave of Christ: A New Testament Metaphor for Total Devotion to Christ* (Downers Grove, IL: InterVarsity, 1999)
Harris, *Tough Texts*	M. J. Harris, *Navigating Tough Texts: A Guide to Problem Passages in the New Testament.* Vol. 1 (Bellingham, WA: Lexham, 2020); Vol. 2 (Bellingham, WA: Lexham, 2023)
HCSB	Holman Christian Standard Bible (2001)
JB	The Jerusalem Bible (1966)

KJV	King James Version (= Authorised Version) (1611)
Knox	R. A. Knox, *The New Testament* (reprint 1997)
lit.	literal(ly)
LEB	Lexham English Bible (NT, 2010; OT, 2011)
LSB	Legacy Standard Bible (2021) (= updated NASB)
LSJ	H. G. Liddell and R. Scott, *A Greek-English Lexicon*, 9th ed., revised by H. S. Jones et al. (Oxford: Clarendon,1940). *Supplement*, edited by E. A. Barber et al. (Oxford: Clarendon, 1968)
LXX	Septuagint (= Greek Old Testament)
mg	margin
Moffatt	J. Moffatt, *The Moffatt Translation of the Bible* (1935)
MSG	E. Peterson, *The Message: The Bible in Contemporary Language* (Colorado Springs: NavPress, 2002)
NAB1	New American Bible (1970)
NAB2	New American Bible: Revised New Testament (1986)
NASB	New American Standard Bible (1977) (see LSB)
NCV	New Century Version (1987)
NEB	New English Bible (1970)
NIV	New International Version (2011)
NJB	New Jerusalem Bible (1985)
NKJV	New King James Version (1982)

NLT	New Living Translation of the Bible (1996)
NRSV	New Revised Standard Version (1989)
NT	New Testament
OED	*The Oxford English Dictionary* (reprint, Oxford: Clarendon, 1961; originally published 1933)
OT	Old Testament
passim	(Latin) in many places
Phillips	*The New Testament in Modern English* (London: Bles/Collins, 1958)
REB	Revised English Bible (1990)
RSV	Revised Standard Version of the Bible (1952)
RV	Revised Version (New Testament) (1881)
TCNT	Twentieth Century New Testament (1904)
TDNT	G. Kittel and G. Friedrich, eds., *Theological Dictionary of the New Testament*, 9 vols. (Grand Rapids: Eerdmans, 1964–74)
TEV	Today's English Version of the New Testament (1966)
TNIV	Today's NIV (2005)
viz	*videlicet* (Latin), namely
vs.	*versus* (Latin), against
Weymouth	R. F. Weymouth, *The New Testament in Modern Speech*, 3rd ed. (London: Clarke, 1909)

Chapter 1

The Genesis and Development of the NIV

BIRTH AMID LAUGHTER

WE NATURALLY ASSOCIATE BIRTH with excruciating pain and a maternity ward in a hospital. So how did a monumentally important birth take place in the Multnomah Hotel in Portland, Oregon, in 1955—prompted by an explosion of laughter? A birth, in fact, that led to the eclipse of a world record that had stood for three hundred and seventy-five years!

A Christian businessman named Howard Long who worked for General Electric was on one occasion dining with a fellow businessman in this historic Portland hotel, and, as always, he was keen to discuss spiritual issues and to share the good news. After the meal Long began to read aloud to his friend from his copy of the Scriptures—the King James Version. When Long glanced up to see how the man was reacting to God's word, he was confronted by an explosion of laughter. Seventeenth-century English sounded like a strange foreign language! We do not know what passage Long was reading out, but it may have been verses like Rom 10:9–10 that summarize the gospel in Elizabethan English: "If thou shalt confess with thy mouth the Lord Jesus, and shalt believe in thine heart that God hath raised him from the dead, thou shalt be saved. For with the heart man believeth unto righteousness; and with the mouth confession is made unto salvation." (Long died on July 31, 1990, at the age of seventy-eight.)

This embarrassing encounter brought to birth in Long's thinking a desire that people everywhere who spoke English should have available a version of the Bible that they could easily understand along with their children. So he shared his frustrations as a keen evangelist with the Reverend Peter De Jong, the pastor of the Christian Reformed Church (CRC) he attended in Seattle, Washington. Then began a prolonged set of negotiations over ten years involving recommendations to the CRC synod, the appointment in 1956 of a study committee consisting of the four faculty members of the Old and New Testament Departments of Calvin Seminary, the rejection of their recommendations by the advisory committee of the synod in 1957, and the persuasive intervention of John Stek (one of those Calvin Seminary professors) that resulted in the **CRC synod of 1958** finally approving the study committee's recommendation that a translation project should be established. These four professors then began discussions with other evangelical scholars and with the National Association of Evangelicals (NAE), which had appointed its own committee "to study the question of the NAE's participation in the possible project of a new English translation of the Old and New Testaments." In 1961 at Grand Rapids an informal meeting took place between the CRC and NAE committees.

But it was not until **August 1965** that an interdenominational group of evangelical Christian leaders and scholars met for two days at Trinity Christian College in Palos Heights, Illinois. Their verdict? "It is the sense of this assembly that the preparation of a contemporary English translation of the Bible should be undertaken as a collegiate endeavor of evangelical scholars." As a result of that conference on Bible translation, a Committee of Fifteen (thereafter called the Committee on Bible Translation, CBT) was convened in December 1965 at Nashville, Tennessee, and they met in Chicago in March 1966 to prepare for the General

Conference on Bible Translation. This major conference was held in **August 1966** at Moody Church in Chicago, with eighty persons in attendance—fifty denominational leaders and representatives of Christian organizations, along with thirty biblical scholars from a wide variety of colleges and seminaries.[1]

Illustration 1: The "Committee of Fifteen" (the initial Committee on Bible Translation), with Dr. Edwin H. Palmer, full-time executive secretary

1. This summary of the early history of the NIV is largely dependent on "Made to Read: The Necessity of the NIV" (https://www.thenivbible.com/50th-anniversary/made-to-read/howard-long); Michael Williams, "Where Did the NIV Come From?" (https://www.thenivbible.com/blog/where-did-the-niv-come-from); and *The Story of the New International Version* (East Brunswick, NJ: New York International Bible Society, 1978). The developed metaphor regarding birth is mine.

Illustration 2: The Committee on Bible Translation (1986), left to right: John Stek, Bruce Waltke, Larry Walker, Walter Liefeld, Ken Barker, Ron Youngblood, Laird Harris, unidentified member, Donald Madvig, Dick France, Donald Wiseman, Murray Harris, Dick Longenecker

FINANCIAL CHALLENGES

Now that the prolonged pregnancy was over, who would pay for the actual birth of the new Bible after its conceptual birth in Portland? In 1968 the New York Bible Society (NYBS, now known as Biblica) volunteered to underwrite the estimated $850,000 (about $7.3 million in 2023!) needed to complete the project. Committed as they were to the exciting project, the society management mortgaged their office space in Manhattan and New Jersey, moved to cheaper quarters in New Jersey, and reduced their staff numbers from fifty-four to thirty-four. Some even took out second mortgages on their own homes. In 1973 the New Testament part of the NIV was published by Zondervan Bible Publishers.

In a letter sent to all of us translators in **February 1974**, Dr. Edwin H. Palmer, the full-time executive secretary of the NIV, gave a sample of the very positive assessments of the NIV New Testament provided by well-known figures in the evangelical world, such as Curtis Vaughan, Elton Trueblood, Gladys Hunt, Billy Graham, Calvin Linton, and F. F. Bruce. But the second part of the eight-page letter was profoundly disturbing.

"The total cost of the project so far—the entire New Testament and part of the Old Testament—is $687,617. But the income has been only $111,967. Thus there has been a loss of $575,650 [about $3.5 million in 2023] to date." Palmer reported that this deficit had been met by a bank loan at 10.25 percent, and the Zondervan Corporation had provided an advance on royalties as a loan, while the balance had been borrowed from other Bible Society designated funds.

In great detail Palmer assessed the cost over the coming four summers to complete the rest of the NIV. He worked out how many verses remained to be completed by each of the four committees—the main Committee on Bible Translation (CBT, all professors) and the three smaller Initial, General, and Intermediate Committees (see below, "Stages in the Production of the NIV," for the interrelation of these committees)—and the number of verses per hour that each committee could reasonably be expected to complete on the basis of their past record. His new proposal was (1) that the committees should work for ten consecutive weeks during the next four summers in Europe (cheaper than in the US); and (2) that a "450 Club" be formed in which 450 people or organizations commit to contributing $250 a year for four years, for the estimated $450,000 (about $2.74 million in 2023) needed to complete the project. In Palmer's heartfelt plea for supporters, he emphasized the uniqueness of the project. "It comes only once. And when you support it, you are not supporting a temporary program, but a lasting one. People forget sermons and church programs, but the Word of God goes on forever."

About nine months later, **November 22, 1975**, Dr. Palmer sent out another letter to NIV editors. The NYBS had just called a special meeting of the CBT, sharing some of the current "frightening figures" and observing that at the rate the CBT was translating, the whole project would not be finished before 1979.

Here are some of those "frightening figures" (even in 1975 figures!).

The Bible Society had borrowed $754,783 and had a "demand loan" of $205,000.

The interest on its NIV debt of $646,483 was up to 9 percent.

The Society had reduced its staff from fifty-four to twenty-six, primarily because of the NIV.

So the options were: abort? Or struggle? Providentially, the society boldly opted for the latter option, but suggested (1) that the General Editorial Committee be discontinued; (2) that CBT should increase its pace over the next two summers, aiming to finish by December 1977; (3) that some may be able to defer payment for services or offer loans to the society; and (4) that more "450 Club" members be sought and fund-raising dinners be held.

It is salutary for all those who have benefitted from the use of the NIV since 1978 to recognize the massive financial challenges faced and sacrifices made during those early years (1965–78), especially by the New York Bible Society but also by all the NIV translators, the financial supporters, and the Committee on Bible Translation (CBT). God's providential guidance and provision are to be celebrated. Edwin Palmer's motto from the beginning had been *Nisi Dominus frustra* (lit. "Unless the Lord . . . in vain"), "Unless the Lord builds the house, the builders labor in vain. Unless the Lord watches over the city, the guards stand watch in vain" (Ps 127:1).

In 1988 the New York Bible Society was renamed as the International Bible Society (IBS, now Biblica) to reflect its international ministry in translating and distributing the Scriptures.

The copyright to the NIV is owned by Biblica, which grants commercial publishing rights to two groups, Hodder and Stoughton for distribution in the UK and Europe, and Zondervan for distribution in the US and the rest of the world. But neither Biblica nor any of its licensed publishing partners has the right to alter the text of the NIV, a right that belongs exclusively to the CBT (see under "Stages in the Production of the NIV" below). This protects the text from external influences such as theological agenda.

TIMELINE FOR THE NIV

1955	Howard Long shares his longing for a contemporary English translation with his Christian Reformed Church in Seattle, Washington.
1965	The "Committee of Fifteen" (now called the Committee on Bible Translation, CBT) is formed.
1968	The New York International Bible Society (NYIBS) agrees to sponsor the project.
1969	*The Gospel According to John* is published.
1971	Zondervan Publishing House becomes the sole American distributor of the NIV.
1973	The New Testament part of the NIV is published.
1978	The complete NIV is published in an American edition and a British and Commonwealth edition (see below). The initial print run of over one million copies sells out before the printing is complete, owing to the success of the 1973 New Testament edition and the wide range of evangelical denominations, colleges, and seminaries that endorsed and embraced the NIV as their official Bible translation.
1984	A second edition of the NIV is published.
1985	NIV Study Bible is published.
1996	The NIrV (or NIRV) is published (see below).
1999	The Spanish NVI Bible is published.
2005	The TNIV (Today's NIV) is published (the NT part had appeared in 2001), with various "gender-neutral" adjustments.
2011	A third edition of the NIV is published, replacing the 1984 and TNIV editions but incorporating about 95 percent of their wording.

Coincidentally, this revision of the NIV was published exactly four hundred years after the KJV appeared (1611).

The two major NIV revisions (1984 and 2011) aimed at reflecting developments in biblical scholarship, changes in English usage, and a desire for increased clarity of diction.

Illustration 3: Leather-bound copies of the NIV 1973 and 1978 editions gifted to translators

The NIRV

Whereas the NIV was aimed at a seventh-grade reading level, the NIV Readers' Edition is designed for readers at a third-grade reading level, which will include many readers whose native language is not English. This version is basically a simplification of the standard NIV, with necessary changes in sentence structure, grammar, and word selection for this specialized audience. Many such changes were recommended by literary experts and by educators specializing in elementary education, but in every case the accuracy, clarity, and readability of the NIV were retained. Many of the NIV translators were also involved in the production of this simplified version that was finally approved by a review committee of the CBT. In total, almost forty people representing some fourteen denominations participated in the production. Because the NIRV is based on the NIV, readers of the NIRV can easily transition to the standard version as their reading skills in English improve.

The British and Commonwealth Edition

Even before the publication of the RSV New Testament in 1946 there was recognition among evangelical scholars in Britain that a fresh contemporary version of the Scriptures was needed. Prominent among those scholars was Dr. William J. Martin of the University of Liverpool, who subsequently became one of the initial "Committee of Fifteen" (later the Committee on Bible Translation).

When in 1977 it was decided that a British edition of the NIV should appear at the same time as the US version of 1978, a committee was formed (later called a subcommittee of the CBT) under the chairmanship of Professor Donald J. Wiseman of the University of London to carry out the "Anglicization" of the final revised copy of the text. This Anglicization involved the adoption of spelling, vocabulary, and idioms that are common in British as opposed to American usage. Such changes, although numerous, are minor and do not compromise the meaning or literary style of the text. In spite of some unavoidable delays, this British version of the NIV was published on February 28, 1979, and was celebrated in a special service of thanksgiving and dedication.

Examples of these Anglicizations include the following: spelling changes such as "neighbour" for "neighbor," "traveller" for "traveler," or "worshipped" for "worshiped"; vocabulary changes such as "cock" for "rooster"; idioms such as "put . . . on bail" for the American "made . . . post bond," or "be given to him" for "be given him."

Illustration 4: British Subcommittee of the CBT (1984), left to right: Howard Marshall, Earle Kalland, Donald Wiseman, Murray Harris, Martin Selman

STAGES IN THE PRODUCTION OF THE NIV

a. Individual biblical books or groups of books were assigned to teams of two to four persons (an **Initial Committee**) that worked at the rate of about three verses an hour.

b. An **Intermediate Editorial Committee** (usually of five) reviewed this initial draft, working at roughly five verses an hour.

c. A **General Editorial Committee** (between eight and twelve persons representing the whole spectrum of Evangelicals) reviewed the tentative final translation of the particular book or books, and experts in English style and idiom and a wide range of general readers (such as students, housewives, pastors and parish ministers, children, and older folk) offered proposals for improvement.

d. The **Committee on Bible Translation (CBT)**, the self-governing executive committee responsible for the NIV text, usually consisted of fifteen scholars who represented a range of denominations and nationalities and were all convinced of the infallibility and authority of the Scriptures. Even now the committee meets annually to discuss advances in biblical scholarship, new archaeological discoveries, and changes in English idiom and style. This committee is independent of any external pressures, and they alone endorse any version of the text that is to be published. But they have always welcomed suggestions for improvement that may come from the committee members themselves (see illustration 8 below) or from any source such as other scholars, denominational representatives, pastors, or the wider reading public. In the early years such suggestions were usually vetted and evaluated by committees (b) and (c) before being presented to the CBT.

At every stage all the major Protestant denominations were represented in the committees. This ensured that the translation was free of sectarian bias and paved the way for its acceptance by a wide range of churches. Little did we translators know as we labored away at our pleasant and enriching task that in the Lord's gracious providence this rendition of Scripture would by the mid-1980s become the most widely owned and used of any translation of Scripture in any of the world's languages.

All those engaged in the translation process received the comprehensive ten-page NIV Translators' Manual (produced by the CBT and adopted November 29, 1968) that outlined the aim, procedure, and principles of the translation, with copious specific examples of appropriate decisions regarding English usage. Also, all translators subscribed to the statement of the Lausanne Covenant on the authority and power of the Bible or to a comparable document.

To indicate the complex arrangements for committee work and the involvement of scholars from a variety of institutions, reference may be made to the Intermediate Editorial Committee of 1971. They met once in spring at Wheaton College in Illinois and once in August at Gordon-Conwell School of Theology in South Hamilton, Massachusetts. (Because most of the participants in NIV translation work were professors from institutions, meetings took place almost exclusively during vacations, especially during the summer months.) In the work of this one committee in 1971, over twenty-five professors were involved from sixteen institutions. They were divided into six sections, three for each Testament, and were reviewing the translations from the initial translation teams.

The net result of this four-tiered structure of translation is that a phenomenal amount of time was invested in the production of the NIV. One circumspect estimate suggests that more than 170 man-hours were spent on each chapter of the Bible, with a total of over 200,000 man-hours for the whole Bible.[2] Such an investment in making a single book available to all-comers is probably without parallel in the history of literature.

The CBT now meets annually and includes women and international scholars from India and Africa. As it happens, the current distinguished chairman of CBT, Dr. Douglas J. Moo, was a student of mine in the mid-1970s, taking my classes in advanced Greek exegesis, Greek grammar, and the Septuagint (LXX).

---

2. Ronald Youngblood, *The Standard* (Nov. 1988), 17.

Chapter 2

Personal Involvement in the NIV

ALL WILL AGREE THAT there are four ideal qualifications for any translator.

- Specialized knowledge of the source language, including a conversational ability in the language if it is currently being spoken

- Previous experience in translating this language

- Being a native speaker of the receptor language, with an awareness of changes in that language during recent decades

- Intellectual integrity, commitment to translating the text as it stands, irrespective of one's view of the content

(The "source language" is the language of the text being translated, while the "receptor language" is the language into which a translation is being made.)

One of the most treasured memories of my academic career is my involvement with the NIV. I am not sure who it was who recommended me to the central CBT, but I have reason to assume it was my friend and colleague at the time at Trinity Evangelical Divinity School in Deerfield, Illinois—Dr. Richard N. Longenecker, one of the founding members of the CBT—for he with others had already proposed my name for the Trinity post that I held for nineteen years. Perhaps Dr. Longenecker's proposal was supported by the fact that I am a New Zealander—after all, it is the New *International* Version, not only designed for an international audience but prepared by international scholars. Some Australians working with Dr. Leon Morris in Melbourne and Professor E. M. Blaiklock and Rev. Francis Foulkes in New Zealand were involved at various stages of the translation process, but I was the only person from Australia or New Zealand to serve on the CBT.

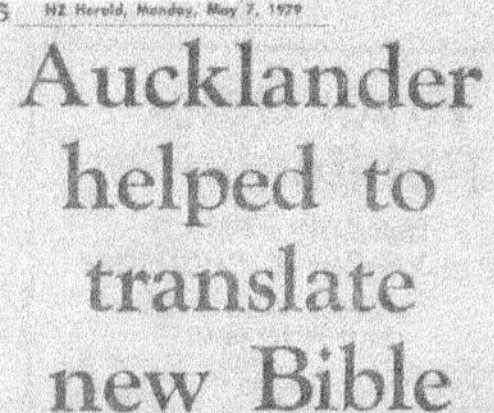

6   NZ Herald, Monday, May 7, 1979

Aucklander helped to translate new Bible

THE PUBLICATION of the New International version of the Bible in New Zealand this year is awaited with considerable interest.

There has been local involvement in its preparation at various stages, for three New Zealanders, Professor E. M. Blaiklock, Dr Murray J. Harris and the Rev Francis Foulkes, all of Auckland, have played significant parts in its translation.

The production of the Bible began in 1968, although its planning had begun three years earlier, and the project was sponsored financially by the New York International Bible Society.

In 1973 the society published the New International New Testament. This latest work includes both the Old and New Testaments.

Commenting on his contributions to this work, Dr Harris said:

"In 1971 I was invited to participate in the project in my capacity as a teacher of New Testament who had a special research interest in the grammar of Biblical Greek.

"A colleague and I at Trinity Evangelical Divinity School in Illinois, where I was teaching at the time, were responsible for the first draft of the translation of St Paul's letters to the Colossians and to the Ephesians.

"This draft became the basis for the discussions of the various committees that checked the translation for accuracy and clarity.

"I also served on the intermediate editorial committee that reviewed parts of Paul's letter to the Romans and the epistle to the Hebrews.

"The publication of the whole Bible gave the opportunity for some minor corrections and revisions to be made in the New Testament (which had been published earlier).

"I feel gratified that some 14 proposals I made (out of 41 proposed, I must confess) were incorporated in the 1978 edition."

Dr Harris and his colleagues worked on the translations at the rate of about three verses an hour — a speed that increased in some committee stages to about five verses an hour. They worked nine hours a day and spent the evenings in preparation for the next day.

"It was exhausting but exhilarating work," said Dr Harris.

Dr Harris was born in Auckland and after attending Auckland Grammar School he trained as a primary school teacher at Auckland Teachers' College, later teaching at Meadowbank and Glendowie primary schools.

When a part-time BA degree in classics had been completed at the University of Auckland he studied for an honours MA in Latin before teaching Latin, English and social studies at Glendowie College for four years.

Meanwhile he pursued his interests in education and theology, gaining a diploma in the former and a bachelor of divinity degree in the latter.

Three years were spent in the University of Manchester, where he was engaged in doctoral research in Bible studies for his PhD. And for the next eight years he taught Greek and New Testament at the Trinity Evangelical Divinity School in Illinois.

For the last three years at that school he served as professor of Biblical Greek and New Testament and was chairman of the New Testament division.

At present Dr Harris is a lecturer in New Testament at the Bible College of New Zealand at Henderson, Auckland.

Dr Murray Harris, lecturer in New Testament at the Bible College of New Zealand, discusses the New International Bible with students Mr and Mrs Edward Sands.

Best seller still gaining ground

THE Bible, in its several versions, continues to hold pride of place as the world's best-seller. It is, in fact, gaining ground in sales.

The "Living Bible," the "Good News Bible" and now the "New International Bible" are some of the more recent editions that give fresh meanings to old teachings.

"Christian books of every description are proving tremendously popular," says Mr E. Bradley-Feary, Wellington-based president of the Christian Booksellers Association of New Zealand. "In the United States there is a boom situation — a trend that is reflected throughout the English-speaking world."

"Here in New Zealand we have about 50 bookshops that specialise in Christian books," he says. "Surely this must place us, on a per capita basis, as one of the leading countries in Christian reading."

Illustration 5: "Aucklander Helped to Translate New Bible" from *The New Zealand Herald*, May 7, 1979 (with permission)

PERSONAL INVOLVEMENT

1970–1971	Original version of Colossians (with Dr. Paul E. Leonard) Original version of Ephesians (with Dr. Richard N. Longenecker) Each pair agreed that I should produce a draft translation of the letter that would be the basis for our mutual discussion and changes or improvements before submission to other committees.
1970	Review of parts of Romans and Hebrews by the Intermediate Committee
1984–1996	Member of the Committee on Bible Translation (CBT)
1984	Secretary of the British Subcommittee of the CBT, designed to convert "Americanisms" into the purity of the "Queen's English" for the Hodder and Stoughton (UK) version of the NIV (see above, ch. 1, p. 9).
1989	(April 24–26 in Dallas) CBT representative at the Spanish NIV Review meeting. As a result of participating in this detailed review of progress, I was able to make formal recommendations to the International Bible Society about the appropriate extent and limitations of CBT involvement in the project, and to highlight the inappropriateness of having persons at Life Publishing who are not experts in Greek make changes in the Spanish NIV from the English NIV. In 1999 a translation team headed by Dr. René Padilla and Dr. Luciano Jaramillo produced a Spanish NVI Bible that bypassed the English NIV.
2015	Published a book entitled *John 3:16: What's It All About?* (Wipf and Stock) that is an exposition of the NIV rendering of this verse for serious readers (with optional technical notes at the end). Copies were made available to New Zealand churches free of charge through the generosity of several trusts and one individual, and hundreds of copies were distributed among students throughout New Zealand by representatives of the Tertiary Students Christian Fellowship (TSCF).
2018	Notes on 2 Corinthians in *Biblical Theology Study Bible* (Grand Rapids: Zondervan; previously published as *NIV Zondervan Study Bible*), 2079–98.

A personal story may illustrate how my happy involvement with the NIV project played out. I was once in a congregation where the pastor was expounding a passage from Paul's letter to the Ephesians. At one point in his sermon he very decidedly declared that the NIV was simply "wrong" in its translation of a particular phrase. The difficulty was that he knew no Greek. Since

I knew him well, I later gently observed that many years ago I had helped to provide the original translation of Ephesians for the NIV. What an embarrassing surprise for him! He graciously accepted my gentle admonition and subsequently sent me a letter assuring me that in the future if he disagreed with a particular NIV rendering he would say, "The NIV translates it this way, but others have taken it in another sense."

QUALIFICATIONS FOR INVOLVEMENT

In my early years my academic focus was initially in classics, so I spent hundreds of hours translating Latin historians such as Livy or poets such as Vergil, and Greek philosophers such as Plato or poets such as Euripides. In that training we were required not only to translate Latin and Greek into English but also to translate English passages into Greek and Latin. Traffic in both directions!

Perversely (some might say) I was fascinated by the grammar of New Testament Greek, and that has become my specialty. But one needs to be very aware of the differences between Classical Greek (about 450 to 330 BC) and Hellenistic or Koine Greek (about 330 BC to AD 330). The expression "Biblical Greek" is the traditional way of referring to the Greek of the Old Testament (Septuagint or LXX) and the New Testament, without suggesting that Biblical Greek forms a dialect of Hellenistic/Koine Greek, which, unlike Classical Greek, is without defined dialects.

One distinctive of my academic background that some may see as an advantage is that all my formal academic training took place in universities (Auckland, Otago, London, and Manchester), either extramurally and part-time or full-time. This purely university pedigree meant that I never darkened the door of a theological institution and so could be neither branded nor dismissed as a Calvinist or an Arminian, a fundamentalist or a liberal, as a result of particular theological training.

During my fifteen years of direct involvement with the NIV, I was preparing material for three books that focussed on the grammar of New Testament Greek and which were subsequently published: *Jesus As God: The New Testament Use of* Theos *in Reference to Jesus* (Grand Rapids: Baker, 1992; Eugene, OR: Wipf and Stock, 2008); *The Second Epistle to the Corinthians: A Commentary on the Greek Text* (Grand Rapids: Eerdmans, 2005; 1,100 pages); and *Prepositions and Theology in the Greek New Testament* (Grand Rapids: Zondervan, 2012) (see illustration 6 below).

So it was perhaps not surprising that I was asked by the CBT after the 1984 edition was published to submit an analysis of how the NIV had translated the crucial verb *pisteuō* (believe) in its various tenses in John's Gospel ("the Gospel of Belief") and in Acts, which so often speaks of "coming to faith" or "believing," and to make suggestions regarding appropriate consistency. Similarly, given my specialized work on 2 Corinthians, suggestions for modifications to the NIV version of that letter were sought.

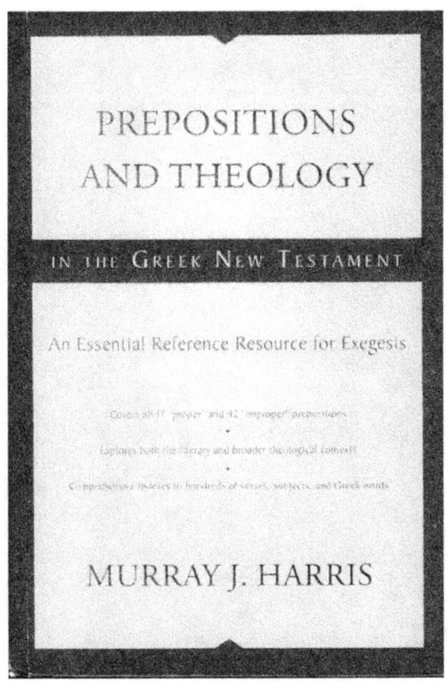

Illustration 6: Cover of *Prepositions and Theology in the Greek New Testament* (2012)

As I look back on my own Christian experience, I was brought up with the KJV as the authoritative version in both home and church, and my memorization of Scripture was from that beautiful translation, which is perfectly suited to be memorized. But with the RSV available after 1946, that became my NT. In fact, my well-worn copy of the RSV NT is one of my most treasured possessions. What the RSV was for young Christians in the late 1940s until the 1970s, the NIV became from the mid-1970s until the 2000s.

Chapter 3

Translation Principles of the NIV

WHENEVER I AM ASKED to speak about the task of translation, I begin with an imaginary story from the previous weekend. Somewhere in Paris a young man, with heart palpitations, reaches into his pocket, grasps an engagement ring, and turns to his young lady friend with the words, "Will you marry me, *mon petit chou*?" How is a translator to render the way he addresses his potentially future wife? Literally, it means "my little cabbage"! What is a suitable English equivalent? A word-for-word rendering might be "my dear one," but that sounds too formal. What about "sweetheart," "honey," "darling," "my valentine," or "sweetie"? No one of these possible renderings can be excluded as inappropriate, but all of them jettison any link with the vegetable garden! True, "my little cabbage" is a local idiom, and the New Testament lacks any comparable local jargon—although it has some disturbingly vivid metaphors, as when the apostle Paul, perhaps borrowing an expression used in an abusive attack on him, likens himself to an "untimely fetus" (*ektrōma*, 1 Cor 15:8; see below in this chapter).

Our English word "translation" comes from the supine form (*translatum*) of the Latin verb *transfero*, carry (*fero*) across (*trans-*), and signifies the "carrying across" or transfer of meaning from the source language to the receptor language. The primary focus in this transference is meaning, but in a secondary sense the translator seeks to reproduce style.

There is a quaint Italian proverb that says, *Traduttori, traditori* (Translators are traitors). What the proverb encapsulates is the truth that no translator can ever do full justice to the text being translated, for no two languages fully correspond in such matters as grammar, word order, idiom, and word associations. So in a real sense, where translators do less than justice, they are "traitors" to the original author and their text. This has prompted the observation that if different translations do full justice to different parts of the text, the distinctiveness of each English version of the Bible lies in the 5 percent that is distinctive to that version, not the 95 percent that it has in common with other versions. There will always be a place for multiple versions!

Translations are often classified in two broad categories. First, some versions aim at **formal equivalence** by using word-for-word equivalents in the receptor language to the extent that such is linguistically reasonable, given the fact that no two languages are identical in grammatical features. The RV, NKJV, NASB, and ESV translations fall within this category. Where there is an emphasis on contemporary readability, some scholars call this **optimal equivalence.** Second, some versions aim at **dynamic** (or functional) **equivalence** by using thought-for-thought equivalents in the receptor language. In this group are found the NRSV, NIV, HCSB, CSV, and NLT. Also included here are the paraphrases or amplified translations such as Barclay, Phillips, and Cassirer.[1]

A more specific classification of translations may be illustrated by citing or giving various renderings of the first verse in John's Gospel.[2]

---

1. See further Mark L. Strauss, *40 Questions about Bible Translation* (Grand Rapids: Kregel, 2023).

2. The following analysis draws on material published in my article on translation technique, "Translating the Bible into English," *Voices* 14 (1988) 12–13; used with permission.

LITERALISTIC

"In beginning was the word and the word was with the God and God was the word."

This artificial word-for-word translation shows the difference between Greek and English with regard to word order and the use of the definite article. If an English version closely corresponds to the Greek, it cannot be in any sense be called a "translation." It is a mockery of the very notion of a "transference of meaning," given the radical differences between the two languages. Only a "sub-text" or "interlinear" rendition falls within this category, but it is not a translation in any sense.

LITERAL

"In the beginning was the Word, and the Word was with God, and the Word was God."

The simplicity and unadorned nature of John's style permit most EVV to provide this accurate and literal rendering. It is sensitive to Greek-English differences, for the two Greek nouns (*archē* and *theos*) that lack the article are appropriately rendered by definite English substantives ("in the beginning" and "God").

But one serious problem remains with this translation. In contemporary English, the word "God" is a proper noun and refers either to the Supreme Deity, however that entity be described, or, more commonly, to the Christian triune God. In the former case, John 1:1b and c would present a contradiction, for the Word could not have been *with* the Supreme Deity and also actually have *been* the Supreme Deity. In the latter case, the Word could not have been in the presence of the triune God and yet also identified with the triune God. But if in v. 1b "God" refers to the Father (as throughout the Fourth Gospel, apart from 1:18 and 20:28 and here in v. 1c), there is no problem in saying that the Word (the eternal Son) was "with God." But in v. 1c "God" cannot refer to the Father, since the Son and the Father are distinct Persons.

The solution has to be that in v. 1c "God" refers to having the divine nature, being fully God by nature, being God essentially. Here in v. 1c, then, the term "God" has a distinctive nuance.

It is precisely this problem that has generated alternative translations of v. 1c:

- "the Word was divine": Goodspeed, Moffatt ("the Logos was divine")

This converts a noun into an adjective, and on either side (vv. 1b and 2), *theos* is substantival, referring to "God" the Father. In modern usage, however, "divine" has a wide variety of meanings (e.g., a divine meal, divine patience). Also, there was available to John a Greek adjective (*theios*) that means "divine," if he wished simply to affirm Christ's "divinity" (however that is defined).

- "the Word was deity": several commentators

The term "deity" (not "the Deity" or "a deity") appropriately does not refer to a person (cf. "God") and does not have a diluted meaning like "divine." But the word has an abstract flavor that does not attach to the word *theos*, and the reader might have expected John to say "the Word *possessed* deity" rather than "*was* deity."

TENDENTIOUS

"Originally the Word was, and the Word was with God, and the Word was a god" (New World Translation = Jehovah's Witnesses version).

From a grammatical perspective, this is a possible translation, because a noun without the article (here, *theos*) may be indefinite. Moreover, Jesus himself reminded his adversaries that God as the Great Judge could refer to the unscrupulous Israelite magistrates and judges as "gods" (*theioi*) (John 10:34–35, citing Ps 82:6) as he was defending his claim to be one with the Father (John 10:30).[3]

3. See Harris, *Tough Texts*, 2:1.18.

But theologically this is an inappropriate translation, for John was a monotheist and so could never describe a single human person as being (using the verb "to be") "*a god.*" This rendering is tendentious because elsewhere in his Gospel, John uses the term "God" (*theos*) of Jesus (1:18; 20:28), thereby unequivocally asserting the deity of Jesus, a truth denied by the Jehovah's Witnesses. So for the sake of consistency, they avoid a translation that could be interpreted as pointing to Christ's deity.

COLLOQUIAL

"When everything started up, the Word was there, and this Word was near to God and was divine."

Even if such a translation were legitimate, it is banal and introduces an English colloquialism ("started up") into a passage that is not written in correspondingly colloquial Greek. There is no "transference of style."

PARAPHRASTIC

"At the beginning God expressed himself. That personal expression, that word, was with God and was God" (Phillips).

Such an expanded or amplified translation seeks helpfully to explain the particular nuance of the rich Greek term *logos*, as the translator sees it—that the *logos* is personal and is a mode of God's self-expression. Both concepts are true and central in John's Christology, but the key term is ever broader than a limited paraphrase could bring out. Jesus Christ as the Logos is the inward and expressed mind of God. It is the role of the commentator, not the translator, to "fill in the gaps" and expound the shades of meaning of key terms.

With that said, there are many places where a paraphrastic rendering is either necessary or perfectly defensible. For instance, in Rom 3:20 the NIV legitimately replaces "[no flesh] will be *justified* [in His sight]" (NASB) by "[no one] will be *declared righteous* [in God's sight]," thus avoiding the technical theological term "justify."

IDIOMATIC

"When all things began, the Word already was. The Word dwelt with God, and what God was, the Word was" (NEB, similarly REB).

Similar renderings of John 1:1c include the following:

- "what God was, the Word also was" (TEV)

- "he was the same as God" (GNB, also another 1966 TEV edition)

- "the nature of the Word was the same as the nature of God" (Barclay)

- "the Word was the very same as God" (Cassirer)

Two features of these "thought-for-thought" translations are commendable:

- They avoid any suggestion of identity between the two proper nouns (such as "the Word was God").

- They properly reflect John's intention—by his omission of the article with *theos*—to describe the nature of the Logos (*what* he was) rather than to identify his person (*who* he was).[4]

However, the idiomatic renderings lack the Johannine succinctness and force. While the NEB, REB, and TEV reproduce the word order of the Greek, they have converted the Greek predicate (*theos*, "what God was") into the English subject.

From this consideration of various possible translations of John 1:1c, we may conclude that the most common rendering ("the Word was God") is accurate and defensible, but it requires that the word "God" is carefully defined or qualified, since in this case it carries a sense that is uncommon in English usage. Not surprisingly, a paraphrase would most accurately reflect the Evangelist's

---

4. For a technical discussion of this issue, see Harris, *Jesus*, 59–67.

intended meaning: "the Word was identical with God the Father in nature."

From this survey of how EVV translate a simple Greek sentence, it is clear how complex the translation process is, as translators wrestle with the Greek text, English connotations, and theological implications.

Most translations fall under more than one of the six categories listed above. The most popular versions, often the product of committees, are both literal (in accurately conveying the sense of the original) and idiomatic (in using contemporary English diction). Translations produced by individual scholars, usually without any official sponsorship, tend to be both idiomatic and paraphrastic (e.g., Moffatt, Phillips, and Cassirer). Their concern to clarify the meaning of the text through circumspect paraphrase accounts for their widespread popularity. The flashes of brilliance and the happy phrases that often mark the work of an individual translator generally find no place in a committee version that tends to have a uniform style that evens out the widely different Greek styles in the NT—one thinks of the unsophisticated and smooth style of Mark or the rugged forcefulness of Paul or the pleasing elegance of 1 Peter.

Quite apart from differences between translations that arise from technique, aim, and audience, other significant differences reflect:

- Slightly different Hebrew, Aramaic or Greek texts

- Differences in punctuation

- Various possible ways of understanding a word or phrase

- Different vocalization (of Hebrew consonants) or even different accentuation (of certain Greek words)

It is often said that there are four ingredients of a commendable Bible translation—the ABCD of translations.

1. Accuracy: a translation should faithfully reproduce the sense of the original text.

2. Beauty: a translation should aim for elegance, simplicity, and timelessness.

3. Clarity: translations should avoid ambiguity (unless intended by the author) as well as avoiding obsolete words and expressions.

4. Dignity: there is no place for passing idioms or slang, but memorable diction suitable for public reading and memorization should be aimed for.

That is, the translator is delicately balanced on a tightrope, striving for elegant accuracy and memorable clarity but at the same time avoiding archaisms and transient modernisms.

All would agree that the primary requirement of any translation of any text, ancient or modern, is **accuracy**, the reproduction in the receptor language of an accurate rendering of the original.

Several general observations about this quest for accuracy may be made, with illustrations from the NT.

1. While a word-for-word translation is often possible (with all the limitations of this technique), *sometimes a paraphrase is necessary*, especially when a technical term is involved.

   - In 1 Cor 15:8 Paul is celebrating God's undeserved kindness (15:10) in granting him a resurrection appearance of Christ that establishes his status as an apostle. "Last of all he appeared to me also, as to an *ektrōma*." Unless we simply transliterate the word (possibly an insult levelled against Paul by his opponents), a paraphrase is necessary. If the term emphasizes prematurity and repulsiveness, referring to an ugly miscarried fetus, a suitable rendering would be "one born abnormally" (NAB) or "one abnormally born" (NIV). Alternatively, if the emphasis is on unexpectedness and untimeliness, a rendering could be "one born out of due time" (KJV) or "one untimely born" (NASB, NRSV) or "(as to) an untimely fetus." Either way, a single word would have been inadequate.[5]

- In its use in the fields of commerce and law, the word *arrabōn* had a dual meaning. It was (1) a "downpayment" or "deposit," the first installment of a purchase, but also (2) a "pledge" or "guarantee" of some type that payment would be made in the future, without being a downpayment. When Paul describes the Holy Spirit as "an *arrabōn* of our inheritance" (Eph 1:14), the NIV aptly renders this as "a deposit guaranteeing our inheritance" (similarly the NIV in 2 Cor 1:22; 5:5). Barclay proposes a similar combination: "first installment and pledge."[6]

- On two occasions Jesus directly addresses his mother using the vocative or address form (*gynai*) of the word *gynē*, "woman" (John 2:4; 19:26). In modern English usage, the address "Woman" often has negative overtones, but in a Jewish setting this Greek form is simply a courteous, formal address, in no way disrespectful. In these two Johannine cases the 1973 edition of the NIV omits the word "woman" from the text, adding in a footnote "Greek '*Woman*' (a polite form of address)." The 1978 and 1984 editions very appropriately render this form as "Dear woman." The 2011 edition has "Woman" in the text in each case, with a footnote "The Greek for *Woman* does not denote any disrespect." In my opinion this is a clear case where a very small addition ("dear") aptly captures the emotive overtones of the word "woman" when Jesus is addressing his precious mother. No footnote is then needed to avoid misunderstanding.

2. Even when a word-for-word rendering is correct, the context sometimes validates an explanatory substitution. As

---

5. See Harris, *Tough Texts*, 2:2.15.
6. See Harris, *Tough Texts*, 1:2.35.

Paul warns the Corinthians in 1 Cor 10 against setting their hearts on evil actions (10:6) and against committing sexual immorality (10:8; cf. Num 25:1–9), he cites Exod 32:6 in 10:7, "The people sat down to eat and drink and got up to play [*paizein*]." While this verb usually means "to play like a child" (*pais*), "to amuse oneself," or "to have fun," in the present context (and see Exod 32:1–14) it probably means "to indulge in revelry" (NIV 2011; earlier editions have "to engage in pagan revelry").

3. In the task of interpreting the NT, the Greek genitive (often translated by "of") is the richest of the cases. It is not only common in the NT but also is capable of expressing many different relationships—such as possession ("belonging to"), source ("whose author is"), epexegetic ("which is"), subjective ("shown/provided by"), objective ("directed towards"), qualitative ("characterized by"), or partitive ("that forms part of"). When there is reason to believe that more than one type of genitive is involved (e.g., Rom 16:26, *hypakoēn pisteōs*, "the obedience that comes from faith" or "the obedience that is faith"), the ambiguous "of" option should perhaps be retained (here "the obedience of faith"—see NIV 2011 text and footnote); but in many cases an expanded translation that indicates the type of genitive is helpful as well as defensible. For example, in 1 Thess 1:3 it is preferable to replace "your work of faith and labor of love and steadfastness of hope" (NRSV) by "your work produced by faith, your labor prompted by love, and your endurance inspired by hope" (NIV).

4. The same principle applies to prepositions and tenses in Greek. Consider the most common preposition (*en*). In many cases a word-for-word rendering of "in" is suitable. But there is a vast array of variations that are prompted by the context and are to be preferred—such as "*by* [the application of] fire" (1 Cor 3:13), "*at* [the sounding of] the last trumpet" (1 Cor 15:52), "*among* the rulers of Judah" (Matt 2:6), "*with* full power" (Col 1:11), "*because of* their many words"

(Matt 6:7), "*with* a promised attached" (Eph 6:2), "*while* un-circumcised" (1 Cor 7:18), "*with regard to* food and drink" (Col 2:16). In the same way, Greek tenses inspire a variety of renditions. Note, for instance, the progressive present tense in 2 Cor 2:15, "We are the sweet fragrance of Christ ascending to God among those who are being saved and those who are perishing"; or the "ingressive" aorist in the Bible's shortest verse, John 11:35, "Jesus burst into tears" (cf. NRSV, "Jesus began to weep").[7]

What I have sought to establish here is that while **accuracy** is the principal aim of any translation of any ancient or modern document, the way to achieve this is diverse—it may come by a word-for-word rendition with innumerable variations (see nos. 3 and 4 above) or by a short or longer paraphrase or addition (no. 1) or by elucidation (no. 2).

7 See Harris, *Tough Texts*, 1:1.42.

Chapter 4

Functioning of the Committee on Bible Translation (CBT)

FOR THE OT THE standard text translated was the latest edition of the *Biblia Hebraica*, while for the NT the textual basis was the latest editions of the Nestle-Aland/United Bible Societies' Greek New Testament.[1]

By the time translation proposals reached the CBT, a lengthy and thorough procedure involving various other committees had been followed (see ch. 1, "Stages in the Production of the NIV").

There are several benefits in the committee approach to translation work.

- No one scholar could ever be completely up to date with the relevant latest developments in the understanding of biblical studies, be it in the field of historical and social backgrounds, literary theory, textual criticism, or the grammar of Aramaic, Hebrew, and Greek. When the expertise of scholars in the wide array of relevant fields is pooled, the translation that results must be more satisfactory than one that depends on the scholarship of a single person.

- Personal preferences or partiality of an ecclesiastical or theological nature are avoided in a committee enterprise.

1. See the preface to the NIV 2011, vii.

Functioning of the Committee on Bible Translation (CBT)

- In the back-and-forth of open and vigorous committee dialogue, problems in the text are more readily solved than in private study and reflection—and new and profitable understandings of the text sometimes emerge.

- Another advantage of committee work, often unrecognized, is that participants are kept humble. When you are teaching undergraduates or even graduates in a formal class setting, there is usually little opportunity for student reaction to what is said, and the instructor is normally regarded as an authority on the subject being taught. Only in a doctoral seminar where students themselves are offering papers are students encouraged to question any view expressed by the professor. But on a translation committee, one is with peers who have similar qualifications and experience and often specialist views, so there is no guarantee that one's proposals and defence will sway the judgment of the majority. So committee discussion is beneficial in promoting humility. For example, only seven of my sixteen proposals for the revision of 2 Corinthians (my specialty, with a commentary of 1,100 pages later published) were accepted and acted on by the CBT. Only fourteen of my forty-one suggestions for changes in the 1978 edition of the NT were adopted. Also, after I submitted my requested analysis of how the NIV had translated the various tenses of *pisteuō* (believe) in John and Acts, only seven of my twenty-five proposals were adopted. Of course, this does not mean that any of my suggestions were wrong. They simply did not meet the 75 percent of votes needed for changes to the existing text.

In what follows I am sharing my own experience of serving on the CBT from 1984 to 1996 (when I returned to New Zealand in partial retirement). I assume procedures were much the same as in the early years of the CBT.

We met from 8 a.m. to 12 p. m. and from 1 p.m. to 6 p.m., with short tea/coffee breaks. Each of the two major sessions began with a brief period of prayer, with a brief Scripture reading in the morning. After all, we had not gathered for an all-day prayer meeting or for prolonged Bible study! Yet we were all profoundly aware of the significance of our project and how the lives of our fellow believers would be influenced by our carefully considered renderings of Holy Scripture. We knew, too, that our families and friends and many others were supporting the whole enterprise in prayer.

The committee atmosphere was relaxed, congenial, and invigorating, for we each held our colleagues in high respect, often knowing them from their influential writings. Voting for an original version of the text required a simple majority, but changes to an existing text required a 75-percent vote in favor. I confess that if we were considering an OT verse (Hebrew is not my specialty) and *on a rare occasion* I was unconvinced by the arguments pro and con for a particular proposal so that I was unsure which way I should vote, I would choose to vote the same way as the chairman, Rev. John Stek, whose exceptional translation skills I had come to admire. If there was a deadline that had to be met to accommodate publishing dates, we would, as an exception, meet in the evening, but usually the evenings were spent in our rooms, reflecting on particularly difficult decisions that might need further discussion or preparing for the next day by reading submissions regarding particular verses.

BETHEL THEOLOGICAL SEMINARY—WEST CAMPUS

6116 Arosa Street, San Diego, California 92115-3902
619-582-8188

Ronald Youngblood, Ph.D.
Professor of Old Testament

December 17, 1996

Dr. Murray Harris
Trinity Evangelical Divinity School
2065 Half Day Road
Deerfield, IL   60015

Dear Murray:

Having found out from the CBT minutes of last August's meetings
that you will be relocating in New Zealand, I am now all the more
distressed that I was unable to attend and participate this year.
I always look forward to renewed fellowship with my CBT
colleagues in general and you in particular.

Thank you, Murray, for all of the courtesies that you have
extended to me down through the years. I deeply appreciate
especially your giving my name to Eugene Rubingh, since that
contact resulted in my becoming a member of the Spanish
equivalent of CBT (CTB). I have enjoyed working with the other
members of the committee for the past several years, and it looks
as if we will be completing the NVI by the end of 1997 with
publication scheduled for 1998. Please pray with us that those
deadlines will in fact be met. There is an enormous need for the
Spanish NVI throughout Latin America.

Please let me know if I can be of any help in your future
ministry. I would like to reciprocate in some way for your many
kindnesses to me through the years. May our Lord grant to you
and yours an especially happy Christmas and a satisfying and
productive New Year.

Fraternally yours in Christ,

Ronald Youngblood

Heart&Mind

**Illustration 7: Letter from Dr. Ronald Youngblood, illustrating the warm
collegiality on the CBT**

Committee concentration was intense, but on occasion in the
heat of the moment a suggestion would be made that turned out
to be humorous, and we would erupt in laughter and the tenseness
would be temporarily relieved. I vividly recall our careful discussion of *mēde porneuōmen* in 1 Cor 10:8, when in the cut and thrust
of spontaneous dialogue someone suggested, "Let us not practice

immorality." Of course the verb "practice" may mean "carry out" as when a doctor practices his profession of medicine. But a footballer practices his moves in the sense of "tries to improve." In the natural hilarity that followed we were not, of course, laughing at the sacred text but at some of our puny efforts to render it in our ambiguous language. In this case an appropriated rendering is "Let us not indulge in immorality" (NAB), or "Nor let us act immorally" (NASB), or "We should not commit sexual immorality" (NIV).

So seriously did we regard our task that I remember one occasion when for thirty minutes we discussed whether or not to include a comma! What that particular passage was I do not recall, but the following instance illustrates the significance of a comma. Consider 1 Thess 2:14b–15a, "You suffered from your own countrymen the same things those churches suffered from the Jews, who killed the Lord Jesus and the prophets and also drove us out" (NIV 1984). With the comma intact, Paul could be affirming that all Jews were guilty of killing Jesus, whereas his intent was to compare the present suffering of the Thessalonians with the persecution of Judean Christians at the hands of some of the same Jews who orchestrated the death of Jesus. The 2011 edition of the NIV removes the offending comma.

To illustrate the translation process and show the many differences between an initial draft and the final product, it will be informative to compare parts of our initial drafts of Colossians and Ephesians with the NIV 2011. (A colleague and I had been entrusted with the task of providing these initial drafts). Between the two versions there will have been many hours of evaluation and numerous changes and improvements, not only by translators on the Intermediate and General Committees and the CBT but, importantly, also because of the recommendations of English stylists and general readers, both young and old.

1971 original draft	NIV 2011 (which here is virtually identical with the 1978 edition)

Col 1:19–23	
[19] For God in all his fullness chose to dwell in him [20] and, by making peace through his blood shed on the cross, to reconcile the universe to himself through him, whether things on earth or things in heaven, [21] including you who were at one time estranged from him and enemies in your minds because of your devil deeds. [22] But as it is, he has reconciled you by Christ's death in his physical body, in order to present you holy and without blemish or reproach in his sight, [23] assuming that you continue in your faith, established and steadfast, and are not constantly shifting from the hope contained in the gospel which you heard, which has been proclaimed to every creature under heaven, and of which I, Paul, have become a minister.	[19] For God was pleased to have all his fullness dwell in him, [20] and through him to reconcile to himself all things, whether things on earth or things in heaven, by making peace through his blood, shed on the cross. [21] Once you alienated from God and were enemies in your minds because of your evil behavior. [22] But now he has reconciled you by Christ's physical body through death to present you holy in his sight, without blemish and free from accusation—[23] if you continue in your faith, established and firm, and do not move from the hope held out in the gospel. This is the gospel that you heard and that has been proclaimed to every creature under heaven, and of which I, Paul, have become a servant.

1971 original draft	Here, too, the 2011 and 1978 versions are virtually identical, except that "men" becomes "people" and "he" becomes "they" in the 2011 version
Eph 6:5–12	
[5] Slaves, obey your earthly masters, treating them with respect and awe, and giving them honest service, as to Christ. [6] And this, not simply when they are watching as though you were seeking men's praise but, as servants of Christ, do God's will with enthusiasm. [7] Carry out your service with good will, as to the Lord and not simply men,[8] for you know that whatever good anyone does will be requited to him by the Lord, whether he be a slave or a freeman. [9] And masters, treat your slaves the same way, and refrain from intimidating them, since you know that a common Master—yours and theirs—is in heaven, and that there will be no favoritism with him. [10] Finally, find your strength in the Lord in his mighty power.[11] Put on the full set of armor which God provides so that you can stand firm against the devil's schemes. [12] For it is not against human adversaries that we struggle, but against powers and authorities, against the cosmic rulers that belong to this dark age, against evil spiritual influences in the heavenly realms.	[5] Slaves, obey your earthly masters with respect and fear, and with sincerity of heart, just as you would obey Christ. [6] Obey them not only to win their favor when their eye is on you, but as slaves of Christ, doing the will of God from your heart. [7] Serve wholeheartedly, as if you were serving the Lord, not people,[8] because you know that the Lord will reward each one for whatever good they do, whether they are slave or free. [9] And masters, treat your slaves in the same way. Do not threaten them, since you know that he who is both their Master and yours is in heaven, and there is no favoritism with him. [10] Finally, be strong in the Lord and in his mighty power.[11] Put on the full armor of God, so that you can take your stand against the devil's schemes. [12] For our struggle is not against flesh and blood, but against the rulers, against the authorities, against the powers of this dark world and against the spiritual forces of evil in the heavenly realms.

Chapter 5

Examples of the Committee on Bible Translation (CBT) at Work

My aim in this chapter is give you the reader firsthand examples of the CBT at work—not the initial draft groups or the preliminary committees, as foundational and essential as they were, but the small group of between twelve and fifteen persons who toiled together and then gave their approval to the finished product that is the NIV.[1]

In what follows, sometimes the reader will doubtless become drowsy and fall asleep as the committee engages in technical discussion—only suddenly to come awake as a favorite verse of Scripture is being discussed. But whether through sleep or alertness, hopefully you will gain insight into the workings of a small privileged group of people who, with the prior devoted work of hundreds of others, would revolutionize the history of the world's greatest treasure. What will become apparent on the one hand is

---

1. For further details, see Kenneth L. Barker, ed., *The Making of a Contemporary Translation: New International Version* (Grand Rapids: Zondervan, 1986), and Barker's two more recent books: *The Accuracy of the NIV* (Grand Rapids: Baker, 1996) and *The Balance of the NIV: What Makes a Good Translation* (Grand Rapids: Baker, 2000); Richard K. Barnard, *God's Word in Our Language: The Story of the New International Version* (Colorado Springs: International Bible Society, 1989); and Burton L. Goddard, *The NIV Story: The Inside Story of the New International Version* (New York: Vantage, 1989).

the complexity of translational issues, and on the other hand how informed and careful our choices were as members of the CBT.

Members of the CBT were always encouraged and sometimes invited to make submissions on issues of general relevance. Here are two of my submissions.

"HOURS" IN THE GOSPELS

12/31/89

1. "Watches" and "hours" need to be considered together. Both should either be changed to modern time (as in the GNT) or both should be left as they are (as in the NIV and the NAB [1st ed.], for example), rather than "hours" changed to modern time and "watches" left as stated (as in the NAB [2nd ed.], and as you appear to be proposing).

2. Solutions to the problem, here listed in ascending order of preference (from my perspective).

    a. Leave both "watches" and "hours" in the text, but in the four references to "hours" in John (1:39; 4:6, 52; 19:14) add a footnote, "Perhaps—a.m./p.m. (Roman time)," as does the NASB.

    b. Leave both "watches" and "hours" in the text but convert all to modern time in footnotes, with "Perhaps—(Roman time)" for "hours" in John, and "I.e.,—a.m./p.m." in the Synoptics and Acts, as does the NASB. But one must then decide whether the writer is calculating four Roman watches per night (as NASB and GNT assume) or three Jewish watches (evening—midnight—cockcrow)!

    c. Leave both "watches" and "hours" in the text, without footnotes (as NIV). This leaves it to the commentator to reconcile (for example) Mark 15:25 and John 19:14 by pointing to various ways of calculating "hours."

M. J. Harris

SINGULAR AND PLURAL SECOND PERSON IN THE SERMON ON THE MOUNT

12/31/89

Both in Matt 5–7 (and in the Lukan parallels) there is frequent oscillation in Greek from singular to plural in the second person, whether this person is indicated by the emphatic personal pronoun, by the possessive pronoun, or in a verbal form. The second *plural* predominates; but the second *singular* is found (in the Greek text) in reference to Jesus' disciples (Matt 6:9b–13; 7:22 refer to God) in the following places:

1. 5:23–26, 29–30, 36, 39b–42, and in the commandments cited or given in 5:21, 27, 33–34, 36, 39, 43

2. 6:2a, 3–4, 6, 17–18, 21–22

3. 7:3–4

The NIV nowhere attempts to distinguish the singular and plural in English (always "you"!). It would be arbitrary to attempt to do so. It is the domain of the commentator if the target language does not permit the reproduction of the natural distinction of the Greek. Where the target language has the singular-plural distinction of the Greek, and it is not offensive to use the singular, then the translation should make the distinction (as in the standard French translation of Segond, Luther's Bible, and the Vulgate), provided it always corresponds to the Greek.

M. J. Harris

Illustration 8 indicates some of the proposals I submitted to CBT regarding the 1984 edition of the NIV. One proposal was accepted, two were accepted with modifications, and one was rejected. This gives a fair indication of the outcome of submissions made by members of CBT to their colleagues.

Example of proposals made to the CBT

```
John 1:12    NIV  Yet to all who received him, to those who believed in his name

             PRO  Yet to all who received him, to those who believe in his name

             Not only in the past (elabon) but also in the present (tois pisteuousin)
             belief in Jesus entitles people to become God's children.

John 1:18    NIV  but God the only^e ⌐Son⌐,^f who is at the Father's side
                  ^e Or but God the only begotten
                  ^f Some manuscripts but the only Son (or but the only begotten Son)

             PRO  but the only^e ⌐Son⌐ who is God and^f who is at the Father's side
                  ^e Or but the only begotten
                  ^f Some manuscripts but the only Son, (or but the only begotten Son,)

             The NIV presupposes (ho) theos monogenēs rather than monogenēs theos.
             Theos is in epexegetic apposition to monogenēs [huios]

John 20:25   NIV  I will not believe it

             PRO  I will not believe

             The it would be best omitted (cf. 20:29 bis), because of the ambiguity
             of its referent and because in the context belief in the risen Jesus
             or that Jesus was alive should not be excluded.


Romans 3:25  NIV  God presented him as a sacrifice of atonement^h, through faith in
                  his blood.  ^h as the one who would turn aside his wrath, taking
                  away sin.

             PRO  Through the shedding of Christ's blood, God presented him as a
                  sacrifice of atonement, to be received by faith

             Nowhere else in NT is faith (whether pisteuō or pistis) said to be in
             the blood of Jesus.  Moreover when en follows pistis (4 NT exx.),the
             prepositional phrase need not denote the object of faith.  See
             NIDNTT, 3.1212 and Cranfield Romans, 1.201, 210.

             The footnote is ambiguous in his wrath.  Suggest deletion, or change
             of sacrifice of atonement to propitiatory sacrifice in the text.


M J Harris
9.9.85
```

Illustration 8: Example of proposals made to the CBT

What follows are specific illustrative examples (mainly from the NT) of important verses and translational issues that prompted thorough preparation or vigorous committee discussion. Here are CBT members at work privately on issues or engaging in dialogue with each other. Unless indicated, references to or quotations of the NIV are from the 2011 version.

The Translation of כסאך אלהים (*kis'ᵃkā 'ᵉlōhîm*) in Ps 45:7 (Hebrew) (EVV 45:6, LXX 44:7)[2]

No scholar would deny that there are difficulties in construing these two simple words—difficulties such as the anarthrous state of אלהים or its application to a human being, if it is vocatival. Confronted by these difficulties, some scholars have resorted to conjectural emendations of the text, proposing as many as six different proposals.[3] But these are ill-advised counsels of despair.

More commonly, various translations have been suggested:

- "Your divine throne" (RSV, NLT mg), "The throne that God has given you" (GNB), or "Your throne is from God" (NJB)

- "God is your throne," "God is the support of your throne" (Knox), or "Your throne is God [or divine]"

- "Your throne is God's throne," "Your throne is a throne of God" (RSV mg, NRSV mg), or "Your throne will be a divine throne"

- "Your throne is like God's throne" (NEB)

- "Your throne, O God," where אלהים is a vocative (that some render by "O Ruler" or "O majesty" or "O divine one")

This last rendering is reflected in all the ancient versions (including the LXX),[4] in many EVV (KJV, RV, ASV, NASB, JB, NAB, NRSV, HCSB, ESV, NLT), and in many commentators. I have fully considered the four main objections (grammatical, structural, contextual, and theological) to this traditional interpretation.[5]

Of these objections, the most potent is the theological. Given the vigorous monotheism of Israelite religion, would any court poet in a nuptial ode ever address an earthly monarch as "God"? In addressing this objection, the exegete must bear in mind certain facts:

2. Based on Harris, *Jesus*, 187–204.

3. Harris, *Jesus*, 191.

4. See Rahlfs's edition, 152.

5. Harris, *Jesus*, 197–202.

- The king, divinely elected, had a unique role in standing "in the place of God."

- Endowed with the Spirit of Yahweh, the king exhibited certain divine characteristics mentioned in Ps 45. For example, "glory and majesty" are ascribed to him (vv. 3–4a) as they are to God (e.g., Ps 96:6); he is a defender and lover of truth and right (vv. 4b–7a), just as God is (e.g., Ps 33:5; 99:4; Isa 61:8); he judges with equity (v. 6b), as God does (Ps 67:4; 99:4); just as God's rule is eternal (Ps 10:16; 93:2; 145:13), so is the dynasty to which the Davidic king belongs (v. 6a).

- A king of David's line could be addressed as אלהים because he foreshadowed the Coming One who would perfectly realize the dynastic ideal, a godlike ruler who would embody all the ideals described in the psalm.

- The use of "your God" in v. 7 indicates that the king is not Elohim without qualification. Yahweh is the king's "God."

- In using superlatives to describe the qualities and achievements of the king (vv. 2–7), the poet is exhibiting the exuberant style and hyperbolic language of an oriental court (cf. v. 1, "my heart is bubbling over"). But in v. 6 the tributes flower into a divine accolade: the Davidic king is God's personal representative on earth.[6]

In all three NIV editions (1978, 1984, and 2011; the 1973 edition involved only the NT), Ps 45:6a is rendered by "Your throne, O God, will last for ever and ever," although in the 2011 edition a significant footnote is added after "God": "Here the king is addressed as God's representative." This footnote accords with my fifteen-page technical treatment of Ps 45:6–7 in 1992: "In this verse it is a king of the Davidic dynasty who is addressed as אלהים. . . . If this is so, Ps. 45 is unique not only as the one genuine hymn to the king found in the Psalter but also as an instance where the title אלהים is used in direct address to the king."[7]

6. Harris, *Jesus*, 200–201.

7. Harris, *Jesus*, 202, 202n74.

This exegetical finding regarding Ps 45:6 (EVV) is important for our understanding of Heb 1:8 where this OT verse is quoted. I end my twenty-two-page technical examination of Heb 1:8–9 with the two following general conclusions that may be cited in full:

> First, although some slight degree of uncertainty remains as to whether אלהים (*elohim*) in Psalm 45:7 (MT) is a vocative, there can be little doubt that the LXX translator construed it so (see *Jesus*, 203–204) and that the author of Hebrews, whose quotations of the OT generally follow the LXX, assumed that the Septuagintal *ho theos* in Psalm 44:7 was a vocative and incorporated it in this sense into his argument in chapter 1, an argument that was designed to establish the superiority of the Son over the angels. The appellation *ho theos* that was figurative and hyperbolic when applied to a mortal king was applied to the immortal Son in a literal and true sense. Jesus is not merely superior to the angels. Equally with the Father he shares in the divine nature (*ho theos*, Heb 1:8) while remaining distinct from him (*ho theos sou*, "your God," Heb 1:9). The author places Jesus far above any angel with respect to nature and function, and on a par with God with regard to nature but subordinate to God with regard to function. There is an "essential" unity but a functional subordination.
>
> Second, given the vocative *ho theos* in 1:8, it cannot be deemed impossible for the comparable *ho theos* in 1:9 to be translated "O God," but this interpretation seems improbable." (See the appropriate NIV rendering of v. 9).[8]

The Translation of μονογενής (*monogenēs*) in John 3:16

John 3:16 is probably the best-known verse in the whole Bible and has been used by God, probably thousands of times, to bring people to genuine faith in Jesus Christ. At some stage in the translation or review process, the CBT was informed by a certain distributor

---

8. Harris, *Jesus*, 227; Hebrew and Greek transliterated.

of Bibles that unless we changed our translation of John 3:16 to read "his only begotten Son" (as in the KJV), they would discontinue distributing the NIV.

Such a request (or directive) was quickly dismissed on principle, quite apart from any assessment of the issue. We were committed on principle to remain independent of any external pressure concerning a particular translational issue, although we were always open to suggestions for change that were backed up by relevant evidence and were submitted through the appropriate channels. Knowing the importance of this verse, we had already carefully considered the evidence and had agreed on the rendering "his one and only Son," with the footnote "Or *his only begotten Son*" in the 1973, 1978, and 1984 editions. The footnote was omitted in the 2011 edition.

Here is a sample of the research that lies behind the decision of the CBT to render *monogenēs* by "one and only" in reference to Jesus, not only in John 3:16 but also in John 1:14, 18; 3:18; 1 John 4:9. Here I partially reproduce (with permission).[9]

What is the most appropriate translation of this word when it is used as an *adjective* (the five instances listed above plus Luke 7:12)—"only-begotten," "only begotten," "only-born," "of sole descent," "without siblings," "unique," "incomparable," "alone of its kind," "only," "single," or "one and only"? When it stands alone as a *noun* (three times in the NT), the context makes it clear whether the meaning is "only son" (John 1:14; Heb 11:17) or "only child" (Luke 9:38).

This word *monogenēs* is a combination of two words—*monos* (only, unique) and *genos* (descendant, species). So the term can refer to "the only member of a kin" or "the only member of a kind."[10] Although, by derivation, the term is not related to "begetting" or "generation," after NT times it came to be associated with those ideas, because in 1 John 5:18 Christ is described as "the One who is born of God" ("he that is begotten of God," KJV). But in NT use the word is concerned with familial relations, not manner of birth.

9. Harris, *Tough Texts*, 2:1.18–19.

10. LSJ, 1144.

In each of the three uses of *monogenēs* in the Gospel of Luke, the familial sense of the word is clear. The funeral procession that Jesus met as it emerged from the town of Nain was for "the *only* son" of a widow (Luke 7:12). Or again, Jairus's young girl who was dying is described as "his *only* daughter" (Luke 8:42). Then in the third instance, Jesus heals a demon-possessed boy whose father pleads with Jesus, saying "he is my *only* child" (Luke 9:38) (these are the NIV renderings).

When Heb 11:17 says that Abraham "was ready to sacrifice his *one and only* son," the word *monogenēs*, here functioning as a noun with "son" understood, cannot mean "only begotten" in a physiological sense, for Abraham had fathered children other than Isaac (e.g., Gen 25:1–2). Rather, Isaac was his "unique" or "one and only" (NIV) son, in the sense that he had been supernaturally conceived (Gen 17:1, 16; 21:1–3) and was the one through whom God's promises to Abraham would be fulfilled (Gen 26:24).

In four verses in John's writings, the word "son" (*huios*) either accompanies the adjective *monogenēs* (John 3:16, 18; 1 John 4:9) or is assumed (John 1:14). Jesus Christ is God's "one and only" Son. John is emphasizing not merely the uniqueness of Jesus but primarily his being "of sole descent." He is without spiritual siblings and without equals. He is "sole born" and "peerless." No one now can call him brother. No one else can lay claim to the title "Son of God" in the sense in which it applies to Christ; only he could expose his Father's heart for all to see (John 1:18). In this connection, it is profoundly significant that in the First Epistle of John, as in the Fourth Gospel, Jesus alone is "Son of God" (*huios theou*, e.g., John 1:49; 3:18; 5:25; 1 John 3:8; 4:15). John never calls believers "sons of God" (*huioi theou*); they are called only "children of God" (*tekna theou*, e.g., John 1:12; 1 John 3:1–2). To express this distinction in a non-Johannine idiom, we could say that Christ's sonship is "essential," relating to his eternal being, while believers' sonship is adoptive (cf. Gal 3:26, where Paul does call believers "the sons of God," through adoption, Gal 4:5).

Finally, in John 1:18 *monogenēs theos* (the preferred textual reading) probably means "the *one and only* Son, who is himself God" (NIV).[11]

In all four NIV editions there is a uniform rendering of the Greek phrase *ton huion ton monogenē* in John 3:16: "his one and only Son," with the footnote "Or *his only begotten Son*" in the 1973, 1978, and 1984 editions, although this footnote is wisely dropped in the 2011 edition.

Matthew 1:25 and Mark 6:3: Mary's Perpetual Virginity[12]

When Matthew affirms that "he (Joseph) took Mary home as his wife. But he had no sexual relations with her until she had given birth to a son" (Matt 1:24b–25a), does the word "until" imply that sexual relations between Joseph and Mary began after the birth of Jesus?

The prepositional phrase *heōs hou* (until) is a shortened form of "until the time when." When it is preceded by a negated action (here lit. "did not know her" = "had no sexual relations with her"), there is sometimes an implication that the negated action continued after the point of time indicated. For example, when we read in Gen 28:15 (in the LXX) "I will certainly *not* leave you *until* I have done everything I have promised you," we may assume that God did not desert Jacob after the fulfilment of his promises.

But far more often we may assume that the *opposite* of the negated action occurs. In Gen 8:7 (again in the LXX) we read, "The raven went out and did *not* return *until* the water had dried up from the earth." Like the dove subsequently (Gen 8:8–11), the raven apparently did return to the ark. Similarly, in John 13:38, "The rooster will *not* crow *until* [*heōs hou*] you have disowned me three times"; and Matt 17:9, "Tell *no one* what you have seen *until* [*heōs hou*] the Son of Man has been raised from the dead." In such cases, the negated activity ends at the point of time indicated by

11. On all the above issues, see Harris, *Jesus*, 73–92.

12. In the following eleven items, I am reproducing, with changes and by permission, material that appeared in Harris, *Tough Texts*.

the "until" clause, and the implication is that the opposite then occurs. But these technicalities lie within the domain of the commentator. The NIV 2011 aptly renders Matt 1:25a by "But he did not consummate their marriage until she gave birth to a son" (the earlier versions have "But he had no union with her"). Cassirer's paraphrase makes the implication of *heōs hou* (until) explicit: "(He took his wife to his home) while yet refraining from being on terms of intimacy with her until after she had given birth to her son." Would the CBT be willing to follow Cassirer's lead with "until after"?

If Matthew believed in the perpetual virginity of Mary, he would be unlikely to express himself in a way that linguistically points to the probability that Joseph began to have sexual intimacy with Mary after Jesus was born. If he had wished explicitly to assert Mary's perpetual virginity, he could have simply added "or from that time on" (*ē apo tote*) after "she had given birth to a son": "He did not have sexual relations with her until she had given birth to a son or from that time on."

If there is a slight degree of ambiguity on Matt 1:25a regarding the question of the perpetual virginity of Mary, that ambiguity disappears in Mark 6:3. "Isn't this the carpenter? Isn't this Mary's son and the brother of James, Joseph, Judas and Simon? Aren't his sisters here with us?" (NIV). Probably the strongest argument for believing that Jesus' brothers were in fact his *blood brothers* or *half-brothers* (having one common biological parent, Mary) is that this is the most natural way to understand the term *adelphos* (brother) when in the immediate context reference is made to his named mother, her son, and his sisters, as in Mark 6:3 (see also Acts 1:14). Also, if the brothers of Jesus were simply his male relatives or *stepbrothers*, there was a Greek word to convey this—*syngenēs*, "relative," "kinsman" (used in Mark 6:4). If the brothers were simply *cousins*, again a special word was available—*anepsios*, "cousin" (used in Col 4:10).[13]

---

13. See further Harris, *Prepositions*, 262–63.

Luke 7:47: Loving Because Forgiven

There is a fascinating correspondence between the Greek conjunction *hoti* and the English conjunction "because," since both can express proof as well as cause.

Consider these two sentences.

- This woman is happy *because* she has won a competition.

- This woman is happy *because* she is smiling.

Clearly the word "because" does not have the same meaning in both cases. In the first case, "because" introduces the ground or reason for the statement "This woman is happy" and bears the sense "for the reason that." In the second case, "because" introduces the proof or evidence for the statement "This woman is happy" and has the sense "as is shown by the fact that." One and the same Greek conjunction—*hoti*—can express both of these senses of "because."

Luke 7:36–50 records the account of Jesus' visit to the home of Simon the Pharisee that was interrupted by the arrival of a sinful woman. When Simon privately objected to Jesus' acceptance of the woman's effusive obeisance, Jesus addressed Simon with a story about the relation between forgiven debts and the intensity of gratitude and love: the greater the debt forgiven, the greater the loving gratitude. Applying the principle to the actions of the sinful woman, Jesus said, "This is the reason why I tell you that her sins, her many sins, are forgiven—because [*hoti*] she has loved much" (Luke 7:47a Weymouth). Many EVV have the ambiguous "for she loved much" (e.g., KJV, NASB).

If Jesus had meant that great love by humans prompts great forgiveness by God, he would have continued, "Whoever loves little has been forgiven little." But in fact he continued, "Whoever has been forgiven little loves little." And three verses later, he would have said, "Your love has saved you [has brought about your forgiveness]," but in fact he said, "Your faith has saved you." So the proper sense of Jesus' statement in v. 47a is "Therefore, I tell you, her many sins have been forgiven—as her great love has shown"

(NIV 2011) (an improvement on earlier NIV renderings: "—for she loved much"). Great forgiveness leads to great love.

Another example (of many) of this meaning of *hoti* is found in 1 John 3:14: "We know that we have passed from death to life because [as is shown by the fact that] we love each other."

John 19:30: *Tetelestai*

CBT members were fully aware of the rich tradition of the Bible in English. In many places the rich cadences of the past were always present in our memories as the result of memorization in our earlier years. How could we forget the immortal KJV renderings of Ps 23 or the Lord's Prayer? The challenge we faced with well-known verses was when to adhere to established tradition when the unchanged original and modern usage permitted it, and when to depart from tradition in order to bring out the distinctives of the text.

Jesus' familiar sixth word spoken while he was on the cross is an example. For hundreds of years this single Greek word *tetelestai* has been translated "It is finished." Along with the majority of English versions, the NIV did not break with tradition but wisely retained this age-old and appropriate rendering. But what would the alternatives have been? Being in the perfect tense, *tetelestai* presupposes a past occurrence, the end of Jesus' life on earth and his successful completion of his Father's will. But the tense focuses attention on the present results of that event, so that "It has been accomplished," "It is accomplished" (Cassirer), "It is completed" (CEB, LEB), "It is consummated" (Douay-Rheims Catholic Bible), or best of all, "It stands complete" would be defensible translations. Colloquial renderings would be "All is done" (BBE) or "It's done . . . complete" (*MSG*).

Romans 1:17: *Ek pisteōs eis pistin . . . ek pisteōs*

With its three references to *pistis* (faith), this verse presents unique challenges to translators. If Paul is repeating the reference to "faith" in the phrase (lit.) "from faith to faith" to express exclusiveness or for rhetorical emphasis, the general sense will be "the righteousness God supplies (cf. Phil 3:9) is revealed in the gospel as exclusively a matter of faith." The NIV uses a paraphrase: "a righteousness that is by faith from first to last." Cf. GNT, "through faith from beginning to end"; and NLT, "from start to finish by faith."

The second case of *ek pisteōs* occurs in a quotation from Hab 2:4b: "The righteous person will live by his faithfulness." The Greek OT (LXX) rendering of the phrase is "by *my* [God's] faithfulness" or "by faith *in me* [in God]." Significantly, in his citation of Hab 2:4b Paul has omitted any personal pronoun—either the Hebrew's "his" or the LXX's "my" or "in me." This suggests that Paul wants the Greek reader or listener to take "by faith" with "the person who is righteous" and also with "will live" in an intentional double sense.

The only way an English translation could incorporate both ways of construing "by faith" would be by "the person who is righteous by faith will also live by faith." But no translation known to me does so. So most EVV have "the one who is righteous will live by faith" (NRSV, similarly NIV), but a few have "the one who is righteous by faith will live" (NAB, similarly RSV, GNT, NRSV footnote). Both renderings concur with Pauline emphases. The person who has received a right standing before God on the basis of faith will lead a life that is characterized by faith.

1 Corinthians 2:13: Verbal Inspiration

It would be difficult to find another verse in the NT where there is such variation among the translations. This is no reflection on the competence of the translators, but it does reflect the ambiguity of the final three words of the Greek of this verse, where

Examples of the Committee on Bible Translation (CBT) at Work

- The verb (*sygkrinontes*) may mean "interpreting," "explaining," "combining," or "comparing."

- The neuter substantival adjective (*pneumatika*) may mean "spiritual things," "spiritual truths," or "spiritual realities."

- The substantival adjective (*pneumatikois*) may be masculine, meaning "spiritual hearers" or "those who possess the Spirit"; or it may be neuter, meaning "spiritual things," "spiritual language," "spiritual faculties," or "Spirit-taught words."

I believe the NIV 2011 rendering is one of the preferable translations, being fully defensible in the context where the emphasis is on the distinctive role of the Spirit in inspiring the words of Scripture. "This [what God has freely given us, v. 12b] is what we speak, not in words taught us by human wisdom but in words taught by the Spirit, explaining spiritual realities with Spirit-taught words." In the previous verse (v. 12) "we" refers to all believers, who have received the Spirit who comes from God and who enables them to understand what God has freely given them. But in v. 13 the "we" (as in vv. 6–7) refers to Paul himself as the recipient and communicator of "words taught by the Spirit." This is "verbal inspiration," the Spirit's distinctive supervision of the words (hence "verbal") used by the writers of Scripture. Both writers and writings were inspired.

Philippians 2:7: Mode of Kenosis

When Paul wrote or dictated the phrase *ekenōsen heauton* (he [Christ] emptied himself) in Phil 2:7 he never would have imagined the mountain of controversy that the phrase would generate. It has prompted what is called *kenotic* theory, the *kenosis*, and *kenoticism*, all of which seek to answer the natural question "*Of what* did Christ empty himself when he entered human history?" Some have proposed it was the glory of his heavenly existence, or the attributes that relate to creation (omniscience, omnipotence, and omnipresence), or the independent or full exercise of his divine power.

But Paul's concern is to answer the question "*How* did Christ empty himself?" Paul's answer is "*by taking* the form of a slave." Paradoxically, Christ emptied himself by taking on the external appearance of a slave—unattractiveness, lack of distinction, and submission.

There is significant grammatical justification for this understanding. When a finite verb such as "he emptied" (*ekenōsen*) is followed by an aorist participle (here *labōn*, "taking"), that participle can define the means or mode by which the finite verb is carried out: "He made himself nothing by taking" (NIV 2011; earlier eds. simply have "nothing, taking"). Another example of this construction is found in the next verse. "He humbled himself by becoming [*genomenos*] obedient to death—even death on a cross!" (NIV).

God the Father's grand reversal of Christ's self-emptying and self-humbling is announced in vv. 9–11: the elevation of Christ to universal dominion as supreme Lord.

Colossians 2:14: A Canceled IOU

IOU is one of many abbreviations, like IQ or IRS or ISBN, that have become part of the English language. The *Concise Oxford Dictionary* defines IOU as a "signed document bearing these letters followed by a specified sum, constituting formal acknowledgement of debt." The Greek equivalent is *cheirographon*, which by derivation means "something written [*graphon*] by the hand [*cheir*]"—a handwritten document or note of any description. In particular it was a signed certificate of indebtedness in which the signature legalized the debt. The word is not found in the Greek OT and only once (here) in the NT.

In his letter to Philemon, Paul has provided us with a perfect example of an IOU. In the course of interceding with Philemon on behalf of his runaway slave Onesimus, Paul makes a specific request. He asks Philemon to charge to his account any debts that Onesimus may have incurred (Phlm 18). He continues: "I, Paul, am writing this guarantee [this IOU] with my own hand: I myself will repay you" (Phlm 19). This is Paul's signed promissory note by which he formally and legally assumes all the indebtedness of Onesimus toward Philemon.

Here in Col 2:14, the *cheirographon* or IOU referred to is our failed obligation to keep God's law, a debt to God acknowledged by our conscience (see Rom 2:14–15; 3:23). This IOU God has "totally erased" or "canceled." The vivid verb *exaleiphō* means "cancel out" or "wipe away," with the prefix *ex* (= *ek*) pointing to the thoroughness or totality of the cancellation.

EVV have understandably struggled to find an adequate rendering for *cheirographon*. As far as I am aware, no version has used the IOU abbreviation. A single word (such as "the handwriting" [KJV], "the bond" [RSV, Weymouth], or "the record" [NRSV]) is hardly sufficient. Many have therefore resorted to a phrase: "the certificate of debt" (NASB, HCSB), "the record of debt" (ESV), "the record of our debts" (GNT), "the record of the charges [against us]" (NLT). The NIV has moved from "the written code" (in the first three eds.) to "the charge of our legal indebtedness" (2011). My own preference would be "the certificate of our indebtedness."

1 Timothy 2:15: Saved "through" Childbearing

The NIV rendering of 1 Tim 2:15a wisely retains all the ambiguities of the Greek: "But women [footnote: "Greek *she*"] will be saved through childbearing." But what are the ambiguities that prompted the CBT to avoid excluding any exegetical possibilities?

The technical word *teknogonia*, which means "the bearing of children" or "childbearing," is unique in the NT and never found in any Greek version of the OT or in Greek writers before the Christian era. It is highly unlikely that it refers to Mary's being the mother of the divine child Jesus ("Women will be saved by the birth of the Child"). It may, however, allude to the God-given maternal role of domestic management spoken of in 1 Tim 5:14, on the basis of the literary principle (synecdoche) by which the part (childbearing) may stand for the whole (management of the home).

"Being saved" in Paul's use usually refers to being delivered from God's wrath now and at the end (e.g., 2 Cor 2:15; Eph 2:5, 8; 1 Thess 1:10). But it is possible that here the verb *sōzō* (save) has the sense "preserve," as in the NASB, "women shall be preserved through the bearing of children." In this case, God's preservation of women may be from death during the process of childbearing or from Satan's destructive grip and deception (cf. 1 Tim 2:14; 5:15; and also 2 Cor 2:11; 11:3).

Even English prepositions such as "through" can have different meanings in different contexts. Consider the following sentences. "The ship's crew were preserved *through* [in the midst of/throughout the course of] the devastating storm." Or, "The crew were preserved from danger *through* [because of] the careful forethought of the captain." The same is true of the comparable Greek preposition *dia*, which may mean, depending on the case (accusative or genitive) that follows it, "by means of," "because of," "throughout," "by," "during," "after," "for the sake of." In the present case where *dia* is followed by the genitive case, it may mean "throughout the course of," "by means of" (Barclay, "by motherhood"), or "because of."

As we survey all of these competing options for the meaning of these four ambiguous Greek words (*sōthēsetai dia tēs teknogonias*), three main alternatives emerge that may here be expressed by a paraphrase, but all may be accommodated within the ambiguous NIV rendering.

- God will preserve Christian women from death during the dangerous process of childbirth. Cf. Moffatt, "Women will get safely through childbirth."

- God guarantees Christian women salvation at the end as they faithfully fulfill their God-ordained and specific calling that involves (for most) childbearing and domestic responsibilities. Cf. NLTn1, "Women will be saved by accepting their role as mothers."

- God will deliver Christian women from Satan's deceitful snares as they faithfully carry out their distinctive God-given feminine roles in family and home, whether they are married or single.

But Paul adds that this divine salvation or preservation or deliverance will come about provided women continue to exhibit four character traits—faith, love, holiness and propriety/good sense/modesty (1 Tim 2:15b).

1 John 5:7: Three That Testify

"Modern English versions remove verses and passages from Scripture as it was originally given, and their translators will, according to Rev 22:19, lose their eternal salvation." Is this not uncommon accusation a fair indictment, for example, of members of the CBT who gave final approval to the NIV?

First, it should be pointed out that the original text of the NT was not written in English (such as we find in the sophisticated Elizabethan English of the KJV), but in Hellenistic Greek, and the KJV was never formally declared by King James I or any church to be the "Authorised Version." That title was a clever publicity maneuver by publishers.

Second, where there are substantial (and not merely stylistic) differences between the KJV or the NKJV and modern English versions of the NT, it is not a case of modern translations *omitting* verses or passages but of the KJV *adding* those sections from certain late manuscripts. Our present verse illustrates the point.

> For there are three that bear witness *in heaven: the Father, the Word, and the Holy Spirit, and these three are one. And there are three that bear witness on earth*: the Spirit, the water, and the blood; and these three agree as one. (NKJV 1 John 5:7–8)

> For there are three that testify: the Spirit, the water and the blood; and the three are in agreement. (NIV 1 John 5:7–8)

As we seek to discover the original text of the NT (or the OT), we are dependent on the work of those scholars who have the necessary specialized knowledge in the field of "textual criticism"—people who can accurately date the oldest surviving copies of the biblical text, since the original text is no longer extant. The fundamental principle of textual criticism is this: the earlier the manuscript, the closer it is likely to be to the original unavailable text.

In the present case, the earliest Greek manuscript containing the words here rendered into italicized English dates from the fourteenth century, whereas elsewhere in the letter the earliest Greek manuscripts date from the third or fourth century. Probably these extra Greek words (italicized in the translation above) were translated from a marginal note found in early Latin versions of 1 John. "Erasmus felt inclined to include it [this interpolation] (reluctantly) in his third edition of the Greek New Testament (1522) because of an incautious promise he had made, and so it found its way into successive early printed editions of the Greek Testament and thence into the A. V."[14] The addition may have been originally prompted by a scribe who wanted to provide an unambiguous affirmation of the Trinity in one place—Father, the Word (Christ, John 1:14), and the Holy Spirit—which would also supply an appropriate contrast ("in heaven . . . on earth") between vv. 7 and 8.

I will conclude these examples of the CBT's work with two instances of significant changes from one NIV edition to another. Such changes are not, of course, changes from an incorrect translation to a correct one. Rather, they reflect the result of further investigation and discussion of linguistically ambiguous verses.

Matthew 11:12: Violence and the Kingdom

> From the days of John the Baptist until now, the kingdom of heaven has been forcefully advancing, and forceful men lay hold of it. (NIV 1984)

14. F. F. Bruce, *Answers to Questions* (Grand Rapids: Zondervan, 1972), 134.

Examples of the Committee on Bible Translation (CBT) at Work

> From the days of John the Baptist until now, the kingdom of heaven has been subjected to violence, and violent people have been raiding it. (NIV 2011)

The translational issues in this verse relate to two cognate words in Greek (rendered "forcefully . . . forceful," 1984; and "violence . . . violent," 2011).

Biazetai (from the Verb Biazō, "Inflict Violence/Force On")

There are three "voices" in ancient Greek: active ("I grasp"), passive ("I am grasped"), and middle ("I grasp for myself"). If *biazetai* is construed as a *passive* form, the negative sense will be "the kingdom of heaven is being subjected to violence" ("from . . . until now . . . has been subjected to violence"). But this verbal form is normally middle and intransitive with positive overtones—thus "force a way in," "advance forcefully," "make a path with victorious force." Jesus would be saying that the kingdom of heaven was now making dramatic inroads into the realm of Satan, with the new age he inaugurated advancing irresistibly on the present age. A positive sense for *biazetai* is found in Luke 16:16: "everyone is forcing their way into it [the kingdom of God]" (NIV), that is, by determined and energetic action. Compare Luke 13:24, "Make every effort to enter through the narrow door."

Biastai (Plural of Biastēs, "Forceful or Violent Man," the Only NT Use)

Outside the NT this word usually has a pejorative sense in reference to a violent or impetuous person. This will have led the CBT to opt for the corresponding passive and negative sense of "being subjected to violence" for *biazetai*. These "violent people" or "predatory men" may have been (1) Jesus' Jewish antagonists, especially the Pharisees, about whom Jesus said, "You shut the door of the kingdom of heaven in people's faces. You yourselves do not enter, nor will you let those enter who are trying to"; or (2) the Zealots, who wanted to eradicate Roman rule from Judea. In AD 6 the revolt of one such "violent man," Judas the Galilean, was crushed by the Romans (Acts 5:37). Regardless of who these people were, their aim was to create devastating hindrances to the advance of the kingdom. They were trying to plunder (*harpazousin*) the kingdom, to claim it for themselves.

My own preferred rendering of the verse would be: "From the days of John the Baptist until now, the kingdom of heaven has been forcefully advancing, and violent people have been trying to raid it."

Romans 3:25a: An Atoning Sacrifice

To establish my conviction that Rom 3:25 is the most important verse in the Bible and that *hilastērion* is the most important word in that verse, I sometimes jocularly engage in the following crescendo—or diminishing focus.

"Who is the most important author in the NT?" Paul.

"And Paul's most important letter?" Romans.

"And the most important section of Romans?" Romans 1–8.

"And the most important section within Rom 1–8?" Romans 3:21–26.

"And the most important verse within 3:21–26?" Verse 25.

"And the most important word within v. 25?" *Hilastērion*.

In a nutshell, the theme of Rom 3:21–26 is "the redemption that came by Christ Jesus" (v. 24b) or "a righteousness before God that comes apart from the law" (v. 21a). The challenge of v. 25a is how best to translate three expressions.

The first is *proetheto*. A literal rendering such as "[God] set before himself" or "proposed" makes the action too personal, as if God were simply engaged in a personal drama. The verb depicts a public exhibition, open for all to see, so that the NASB rendering "displayed publicly" or the NIV "presented" is apt. Both here and

Examples of the Committee on Bible Translation (CBT) at Work

in Gal 3:1 ("Before your very eyes Jesus Christ was publicly exhibited/clearly portrayed as crucified"), the emphasis rests on the clear and vivid verbal portrayal of Christ's crucifixion or sacrifice of atonement as being at the heart of the gospel.

The second key word is *hilastērion*. In Greek and Roman usage, the term refers to a propitiatory gift or votive offering given to a deity as a way of regaining the deity's goodwill. The distinctive element in the NT is the fact that God himself takes the initiative in removing the obstacle to reconciliation—human sin.

In the first use of *hilastērion* in the Greek Bible (Exod 25:17), the lid of pure gold on the ark of the covenant in the most holy place is described as being "atoning." This cover was the "place of atonement," where the high priest sprinkled blood to atone for the sins of the people on the day of atonement (Yom Kippur) once a year (Lev 16:13–16). This accounts for translating *hilastērion* as "mercy seat" in the KJV (following Tyndale, and Luther's *Gnadenstuhl*) of Rom 3:25 and Heb 9:5 (the only two uses of the word in the NT).

From a grammatical point of view, in Rom 3:25 *hilastērion* could be an adjective (atoning), with *thyma* (sacrifice) understood; thus "a sacrifice of atonement" (NIV, NRSV). If, as in Heb 9:5, it is a neuter noun, the sense will be "means of expiation" or "place of propitiation" (the renderings of the principal NT Greek lexicon BDAG, with the former preferred in Rom 3:25); "a propitiatory sacrifice"[15]; or "a sacrifice by which sin is forgiven."

In English, "propitiate" means "make gentle in manner," and "expiate" means "make amends for." Behind propitiation is the NT concept of the wrath of God. Expiation involves the removal of sin through sacrifice. God is propitiated and sin is expiated; propitiation is through expiation. In other words, God's wrath against sin was averted when he provided (or presented) Jesus Christ as "a sacrifice of atonement" or "a propitiatory sacrifice" or "a sacrifice by which sin is forgiven." Is not *hilastērion* the most important word in the Bible—if we must choose?

15. C. E. B. Cranfield, *A Critical and Exegetical Commentary on Romans*, vol. 1 (Edinburgh: T&T Clark, 1975).

The third expression is *en tō autou haimati,* "in/by his own blood." Since this phrase immediately follows "through faith" in the Greek word order, the first three eds. of the NIV have "through faith in his blood" after sacrifice of atonement." In Paul's writings the word "faith" is normally followed by a person and the genitive case, as in vv. 22 and 26, not by a preposition (here "in"). "Faith in his blood" would be a case of synecdoche (part standing for the whole), where "his blood" stands for "Jesus Christ who shed his blood."

The NIV 2011 recognizes that in v. 25a, as often in his letters, Paul is using separate abbreviated phrases, so that after "sacrifice of atonement," we now read "through the shedding of his blood—to be received by faith." That is, Christ and the benefits of his sacrifice are to be received by faith.

In the second part of v. 25, Paul goes on to observe that the purpose of God's provision of Christ as an atoning sacrifice was to demonstrate his justice or righteous character that needed vindication, because in his patience (not his indifference) God had refrained from exacting the full and proper penalty for acts of sin committed in the time before the cross.

To illustrate the complexity of the issues in this crucial paragraph (vv. 21–26) toward the end of Rom 3, here is a copy of my rough notes from October 1970, when I was serving on an NIV Intermediate Committee that was reviewing the proposed text of Romans and Hebrews. The blackness of the page is witness to the intensity of the discussion.

Examples of the Committee on Bible Translation (CBT) at Work

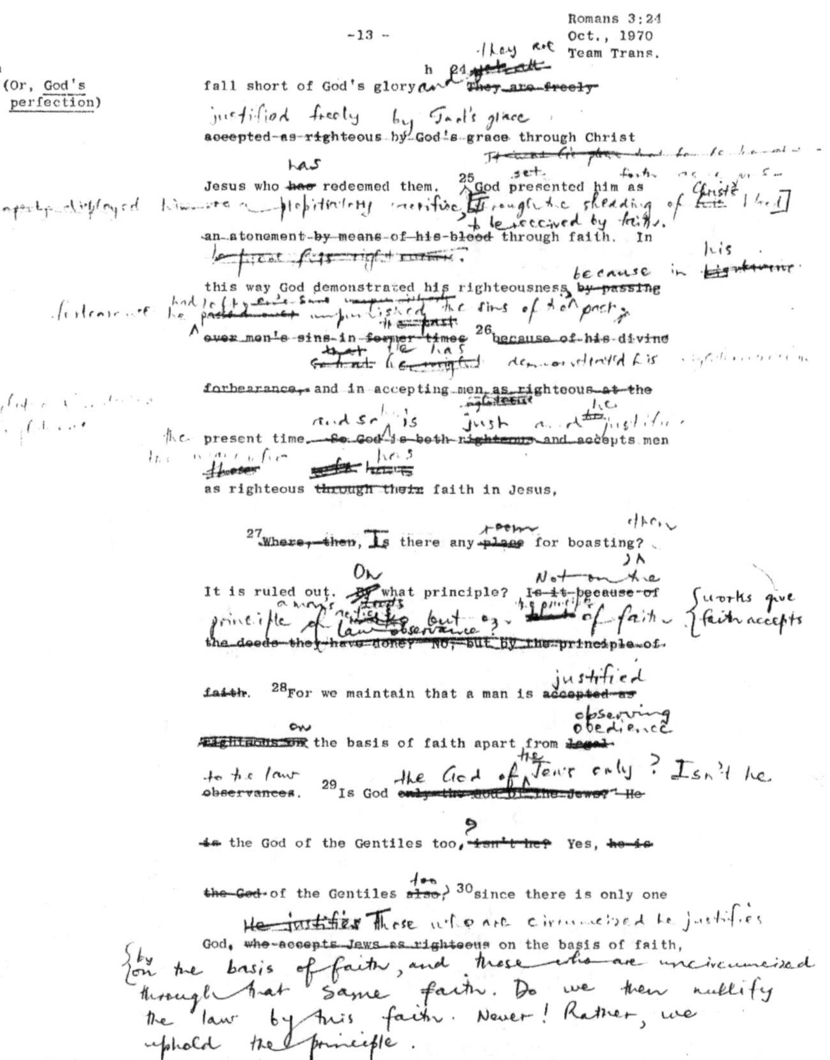

**Illustration 9: My worksheet from review of Rom 3:24–30 by the
Intermediate Committee**

Chapter 6

Evaluating the NIV

It is scarcely surprising that with the widespread circulation and popularity of the NIV there have been a myriad of reviews of this translation since the NT version appeared in 1973. Ever since the TNIV (Today's NIV) ceased to be printed and the 2011 version came on the scene, the predominant concern of reviewers has been the so-called "gender-neutral" controversy.

Reviewers of the NIV seem to fall into one or more of the following categories.

- The ignorant, who declare this or that NIV rendering to be "wrong," when they know nothing of the biblical languages

- The vindictive, who pronounce the NIV to be "perverse" because it deviates in many places from the KJV, or who assert it is "erroneous" at numerous points, especially when it "omits" verses from the inspired text

- The arrogant, who boldly state that a certain translation is simply "inaccurate" or "incorrect," when the Hebrew, Aramaic, or Greek actually permits a variety of understandings

- The insightful, who may or may not have competence in the biblical languages but who recognize that some or many of the NIV's translations are "illuminating" or possibly should be reconsidered

- The commendable, who, from an unbiased and informed standpoint, carefully assess each controversial rendering, or the NIV as a whole, solely on its merits apart from presuppositions

Only those who fall into the last two categories need to be taken seriously.

In the present chapter I shall deal, in admittedly arbitrary fashion, with this most recent inclusive language controversy, then in general terms with the relation between the KJV and the NIV, and finally I will give examples of significant verses where I deviate from the official NIV text. This latter issue will be further developed in the final chapters.

THE "GENDER-NEUTRAL" CONTROVERSY

When the NIV 2011 departed from the 1984 edition with regard to "gender-neutral" language, the translators followed general guidelines such as the following:

- Since sexuality is inapplicable to God, Satan, or angels, references to these figures will always be masculine in gender.

- Masculine pronouns will be used in reference to the Spirit, although the Hebrew and Greek terms for the Spirit are grammatically feminine and neuter respectively.

- Where the context clearly indicates that male or female persons are being referred to, the original reference should be maintained. For example, wisdom literature in the ancient world was customarily addressed to young men about to enter adulthood (thus, e.g., "my son" in Prov 1:8, 15; 2:1; 3:1).

- A gender-specific word may be demanded by the context. For example, note the NIV rendering of *huios* in Gal 4:6–7: "Because you are his *sons*, God sent the Spirit of his Son into our hearts, the Spirit who calls out, '*Abba*, Father.' So you are no longer a slave, but God's *child*; and since you are his *child*, God has made you also an heir."

- Inclusive singular pronouns may be followed by plural pronouns when a subsequent pronoun is needed (e.g., "whoever/everyone . . . they/them . . ."). For example, "*No one* can come to me unless the Father who sent me draws *them*, and I will raise *them* up at the last day" (John 6:44).

The best way to illustrate the issues at stake in this controversy is to compare the renderings of sample OT and NT passages in the KJV, ESV, and NIV 2011 translations. The relevant parts of the NIV are italicized. In addition, to have the ESV and NIV side by side indicates how the NIV has updated English style and idiom, quite apart from gender issues.

Psalm 1:3

> And he shall be like a tree planted by the rivers of water, that bringeth forth his fruit in his season; his leaf also shall not wither; and whatsoever he doeth shall prosper. (KJV)

> He is like a tree planted by streams of water that yields its fruit in its season, and its leaf does not wither. In all that he does, he prospers. (ESV)

> *That person* is like a tree planted by streams of water, which yields its fruit in season and whose leaf does not wither—whatever *they* do prospers. (NIV)

Psalm 8:4

> What is man, that thou art mindful of him? and the son of man, that thou visiteth him? (KJV)

> What is man that you are mindful of him, and the son of man that you care for him? (ESV)

> What is *mankind* that you are mindful of *them, human beings* that you care for *them*? (NIV)

Proverbs 15:5

A fool despiseth his father's instruction: but he that regardeth reproof is prudent. (KJV)

A fool despises his father's instruction, but whoever heeds reproof is prudent. (ESV)

A fool spurns a *parent's* discipline, but whoever heeds correction shows prudence. (NIV)

Matthew 18:15

Moreover if thy brother shall trespass against thee, go and tell him his fault between thee and him alone: if he shall hear thee, thou hast gained thy brother. (KJV)

If your brother sins against you, go and tell him his fault, between you and him alone. If he listens to you, you have gained your brother. (ESV)

If your brother *or sister* sins* [*Some manuscripts *sins against you*], go and point out *their* fault, *just* between *the two of you*. If *they* listen to you, you have won *them* over. (NIV)

John 14:21

He that hath my commandments, and keepeth them, he it is that loveth me: and he that loveth me shall be loved of my Father, and I will love him, and will manifest myself to him. (KJV)

Whoever has my commandments and keeps them, he it is who loves me. And he who loves me will be loved by my Father, and I will love him and manifest myself to him. (ESV)

Whoever has my commands and keeps them is *the one* who loves me. *The one* who loves me will be loved by my Father, and I too will love *them* and show myself to *them*. (NIV)

1 Corinthians 10:1

> Moreover, brethren, I would not that ye should be ignorant, how that all our fathers were under the cloud. (KJV)

> For I do not want you to be unaware, brothers, that our fathers were all under the cloud. (ESV)

> For I do not want you to be ignorant of the fact, brothers *and sisters*, that our *ancestors* were all under the cloud. (NIV)

Revelation 3:20

> Behold, I stand at the door and knock: if any man hears my voice, and open the door, I will come in to him, and will sup with him, and he with me. (KJV)

> Behold, I stand at the door and knock. If anyone hears my voice and opens the door, I will come in to him and eat with him, and he with me. (ESV)

> Here I am! I stand at the door and knock. If *anyone* hears my voice and opens the door, I will come in and eat with *that person*, and *they* with me. (NIV)

It is clear, then, that the changes found in the NIV are designed to communicate the meaning of the text as accurately as possible in current English where the terms "man" or "he" or "brothers" seem to exclude girls or women. To avoid this misunderstanding, the inclusion of women in potentially ambiguous statements is now made explicit. In the current social climate there is increasing sensitivity about gender inclusiveness, but this was not the primary motivation for changes in the NIV 2011.

True, in general usage (especially in poetry, both ancient and modern) the word "man" may refer to both genders, to human beings at large, and to "mankind" or "the human race." Certainly, in formal legal documents "he," "him," and "his" are generic in sense, being comprehensive in referring to both male and female.

But with that said, at the present time as we listen to general conversation or read newspaper articles and popular literature, we discover that broad terms such as "people" or "humans" or "everyone" or "anyone" are regularly used to include both sexes, rather than the generic "he."

Nor should we overlook the fact that the NIV sometimes retains "man" and "he/him/his." For example, Ps 34:6, "This poor *man* called, and the LORD heard *him*; he saved *him* out of all *his* troubles"; and 1 Cor 13:1, "If I speak in the tongues of *men* or of angels." In keeping with its concern to highlight the continuity and harmony between the two Testaments (see above on Ps 45:7), the NIV retains the expression "son of man" throughout Ezekiel (see the footnote on Ezek 2:1) and in Dan 7:13 where the lengthy footnote reads, "The Aramaic phrase *bar enash* means *human being*. The phrase *son of man* is retained here because of its use in the New Testament as a title of Jesus, probably based largely on this verse."

THE KJV AND THE NIV

The NIV **differs** from the KJV in numerous ways.

1. No translation of the Bible into English, such as the NIV, will ever be able to match the KJV for sheer literary beauty, its memorable cadences as "a well of purest English undefiled."[1]

2. No translation of the Bible into English, such as the NIV, will ever be able to match the KJV for its influence on the English language in the area of everyday usage and memorable phrases. Think, for example, of the following expressions: "a pearl of great price," "the signs of the times," "the widow's mite," "stand in awe," "a thorn in the flesh," "the apple of his eye," "precept upon precept, line upon line," and "a still small voice."

3. With the discovery of hundreds of manuscripts containing the Greek of the NT in part or in whole since 1611, the NIV

---

1. Source of this description unknown.

translates a Greek text that is even closer to the unavailable original than was possible for the KJV translators.

It is often wrongly asserted that for the text of the NT, the KJV was based on the *textus receptus* (received text). That exaggerated Latin expression was used in the publishers' preface to the second edition (1633) of the Greek NT prepared by the Elzevir brothers, many years *after* the KJV was being translated (1607–11). The KJV was based on the fourth edition of the Greek NT published by Stephanus in 1551 and the comparable 1588–89 and 1598 editions of the Greek NT prepared by Theodore Beza. All of these editions largely reflect the Greek NT of the Dutch scholar Desiderius Erasmus (1466–1536) that was first published in 1516. The KJV was never officially "authorized" by any authority. It was sponsored by King James I of England who officially appointed the translators. Only the earlier Great Bible in its 1540 edition and beyond was officially authorized by the words, "This is the Bible appointed to the use of the churches."

Erasmus's work on his Greek text was done under pressure, since he was wanting to beat a competitor and be the first to publish a Greek NT. He used the six manuscripts locally available to him, but, unfortunately, none included the entire NT and none predated the twelfth century. His one manuscript for Revelation lacked the last six verses, so he creatively translated the Latin Vulgate version back into Greek. The Vulgate influenced Erasmus elsewhere. For example, in Acts 9:6 the words "And he trembling and astonished said, Lord, what wilt thou have me to do? And the Lord said unto him" (KJV) are not found in any known Greek manuscript (but see Acts 22:10).[2]

For the NT, each of the NIV editions (1973, 1978, 1984, 2011) was based on the latest editions of the Nestle-Aland or United Bible Societies' Greek New Testament, reflecting manuscripts dating from about AD 200 until the invention of the printing press in 1440.

2. See further D. A. Carson, *The King James Version Debate: A Plea for Realism* (Grand Rapids: Baker, 1979), and James R. White, *The King James Only Controversy* (Minneapolis: Bethany, 1995; 2nd ed., 2009).

4. Whereas the NIV was translated into contemporary English of the twentieth and twenty-first centuries, the KJV was translated into Elizabethan or Shakespearean English spoken from about 1500 to 1750. Examples of expressions from Elizabethan English found in the KJV but not understood today in the sense intended include the following: "Thou shalt destroy them that speak leasing" (Ps 5:6); "I prevented the dawning of the morning"(Ps 119:147); "We do you to wit of the grace of God" (2 Cor 8:1); "Only he who now letteth will let" (2 Thess 2:7).

5. In 1607 the task of revising the current edition of the Bishops' Bible (first published in 1568) began, with instructions also to consult the revised Greek text of Erasmus along with the Vulgate and current Hebrew texts. The revision was assigned to fifty-four men in six teams, two meeting in Westminster, two in Cambridge, and two in Oxford. In each team some scholars focussed on Hebrew texts, others on Greek texts. The chapter and verse divisions in the text followed what were first found in the Geneva Bible and copied in the Bishops' Bible. Each team reported to the other teams, but there was no central committee meeting regularly and giving final approval to the published version, as was the case with the CBT regarding the NIV. Moreover, the CBT comprised both Hebrew and Greek scholars.

Remarkably, what the KJV and NIV have **in common** is that their publication immediately prompted vigorous opposition. Hugh Broughton, a notable scholar renowned for his contentious views, had not been included among the KJV translators, so it was no surprise that when this new translation finally appeared he pronounced it to be heretical as well as unreliable. "I had rather be rent to pieces with wild horses than any such translation by my consent should be urged upon poor churches."[3] Compare with this the description of the NIV, this time not by competent scholars, as

3. Hugh Broughton, as quoted in A. Kenneth Curtis, "No Overnight Success," *Christian History* 100 (2010).

"Satan's masterpiece," to be avoided at all costs: "Abstain from all appearance of evil" (1 Thess 5:22 KJV).

One is reminded of the reaction to E. J. Goodspeed's innovative translation, *The New Testament: An American Translation*. In his autobiography Goodspeed reminisces about the furor his work provoked and cites the eloquent outburst of a Dr. Keene Ryan of Chicago: "Theologians and laymen alike will await with awe for God to strike him dead for thus laying his calloused hands upon the Holy of Holies"![4]

Another **similarity** between the two versions is that the translators chosen represented all branches of the Protestant church—in the case of the KJV, both Anglicans and Puritans, "high" churchmen and "low" churchmen; in the case of the NIV, representatives from all Protestant communions, such as Anglicans, Presbyterians, Methodists, Baptists, Brethren, Christian Reformed, Lutheran, Nazarene, or Mennonite.

DEVIATIONS FROM THE NIV

From earlier chapters it will have become apparent to the reader that while I have wholeheartedly endorsed the NIV in its various editions, in not a few places I still prefer other translations of the text. All of us as members of the CBT team were free to express our views about any issue or particular translation, but we were always happy to approve the committee vote, even if it did not reflect our preference. To illustrate this point of personal deviations from the final approved text, I will now discuss two significant verses.

Hebrews 12:2a

> For the joy that was set before him [he] endured the cross. (KJV)

4. E. J. Goodspeed, *As I Remember* (New York: Harper, 1953), 172.

Motivated by the exhilarating and exquisite prospect of providing believers with immediate access to God and of receiving the accolades of the redeemed, Jesus patiently endured the cross.

So well loved is this KJV rendering of Heb 12:2a that it would seem to some to be irreverent to call into question this often-quoted translation. But there are legitimate reasons for doing so.

In the crucial phrase *anti tēs prokeimenēs autō charas* (*anti the joy set before him*), the preposition *anti* may introduce a reason or cause, or may denote substitution.

1. *Reason or Cause*

- "For the joy" (NIV all eds., ASV, RSV, NASB, NKJV, HCSB, ESV)
- "For the sake of" (NAB, NRSV, Weymouth)
- "Because of" (GNT, NLT, Phillips)

On this view, Jesus endured the cross "*in order to obtain* the joy in store for him as his recompense," the joy being his future satisfaction in seeing "the light [of life]" after his suffering (Isa 53:11) and the joy of seeing the positive outcome of his endurance of the cross.

2. *Substitution*

- "Instead of" (NRSV footnote; NLT footnote; and see BDAG and TDNT below)
- "In place of" (Goodspeed)

On this understanding, Jesus endured the cross "*instead of* the heavenly bliss of continued fellowship with God in his immediate presence," a privilege that lay before him as a distinct possibility within his grasp.

I believe this second alternative is preferable for several reasons:[5]

---

5. Harris, *Prepositions*, 56.

- An analysis of the twenty-two NT uses of *anti* leads to the conclusion that apart from the six instances where this preposition joins another word to form a virtual conjunction, it always expresses (15x) or alludes to (1x, Matt 17:27) a substitutionary exchange ("instead of").

- Elsewhere in Hebrews (6:18; 12:1), the verb *prokeimai* (set before) denotes a present reality, not a future acquisition.

- It would seem inappropriate for Jesus' primary motive for enduring suffering to be personal advantage or future reward.

- The two major NT Greek lexicons opt for the translation "instead of."[6]

- The idea of the voluntary renunciation of personal rights for the sake of others is a common NT sentiment (e.g., Mark 8:35; Rom 15:1–3; 1 Cor 9:19–23; 2 Cor 8:9; Phil 2:6–8).

From this perspective, the author is not speaking of Jesus' motivation for his endurance of crucifixion and his scorning of its disgrace, namely, to obtain joy, but is speaking of the disregard of personal advantage that was involved in his steady submission to the suffering of the cross. Jesus was like Moses (Heb 11:25) in that he chose to ignore his own pleasure in order to achieve a higher goal. Jesus was unlike Moses (Heb 11:26) in that his motive for enduring disgrace was not anticipation of a future reward.

2 Corinthians 5:19a

> God was in Christ, reconciling the world unto himself.
> (KJV)

Only one major modern translation (NLT) follows the lead of the KJV and renders this expression in exactly the same way (with "to" instead of "unto"). Several versions follow the RV in reproducing the KJV but omit the crucial comma after Christ (RSV, NASB, NKJV, NEB, REB, NJB, Weymouth). In effect, this omission of the

6. BDAG, 88a, "anti," and 871b, "prokeimai"; and J. Schneider, in TDNT, 7:577.

comma potentially creates an ambiguity, for then "in Christ" can be taken to mean "through Christ," a sense that not infrequently becomes explicit in some other EVV. But when some of the versions just mentioned (viz. RSV, NEB, REB) contain an alternative marginal reading that makes the agency of Christ explicit, one may perhaps assume that the translation in their text should be understood in the KJV sense, but this is not clearly the case.

My reasons for preferring the KJV rendering over the NIV ("God was reconciling the world to himself in Christ") are as follows:[7]

- The periphrastic imperfect construction ("was reconciling") reflected in the NRSV rendering is not common in Paul (only in Gal 1:22–23; Phil 2:26), and when it is found, no significant words intervene (such as "in Christ" and "world" in the Greek here) between "was" and "reconciling."

- The word order of the Greek favors the KJV. When Paul speaks of reconciliation elsewhere, his word order is the verb reconcile—the object of reconciliation—the goal of reconciliation (as in Rom 5:10; 2 Cor 5:18; Col 1:20), not as here the object of reconciliation—the verb reconcile—the goal of reconciliation; and the agent is expressed by "through" (*dia*), not by "in" (*en*).

- In the single Greek sentence (2 Cor 5:18–19) it would be repetitious to express the idea of agency in reconciliation twice ("through Christ . . . in/through Christ").

All will agree that no translation of any text, ancient or modern, is perfect. If so, all translators of the Bible can benefit from perceptive critiques; and perhaps the NIV has earned the distinction of being less imperfect than most other translations.

7. For additional detail, see Harris, 2 *Cor*, 440–43.

Chapter 7

A Perennial Translation Problem

IF YOU WERE (UNFAIRLY) to ask modern translators of the NT to identify the one Greek word that proved the most challenging for them to represent appropriately in English, what do you imagine their answer would be? I venture to suggest it would be the simple six-letter word *doulos*. I remember once seeing on YouTube a publicity session held at the Tyndale House Library in Cambridge (UK) advertising the ESV. And what do you think the viewers saw the translation committee vigorously discussing? How to translate *doulos*!

But why is this little word so difficult to translate appropriately? It is because the associations of the word are so complex, particularly in the US and the UK. All sorts of embarrassing and conflicting emotions are aroused whenever we heard the word. Americans tend to think of Uncle Tom in Harriet Beecher Stowe's *Uncle Tom's Cabin*; or Kunta Kinte in Alex Haley's *Roots*; or their most famous abolitionist, Frederick Douglass. Britishers tend to recall the barbaric slave trader John Newton and his hymn "Amazing Grace" or the tireless efforts of William Wilberforce to abolish slavery in the British Empire in the nineteenth century.

In spite of presenting a requested report to the CBT on the NT use of *doulos*, I was unable to persuade my colleagues to translate *doulos* by "slave" in some crucial passages such as the very first verse of Romans. So strongly did I feel about this whole issue that

I finally produced a book in the New Studies in Biblical Theology series entitled *Slave of Christ: A New Testament Metaphor for Total Devotion to Christ,* various parts of which (usually with changes) I reproduce below with permission.[1]

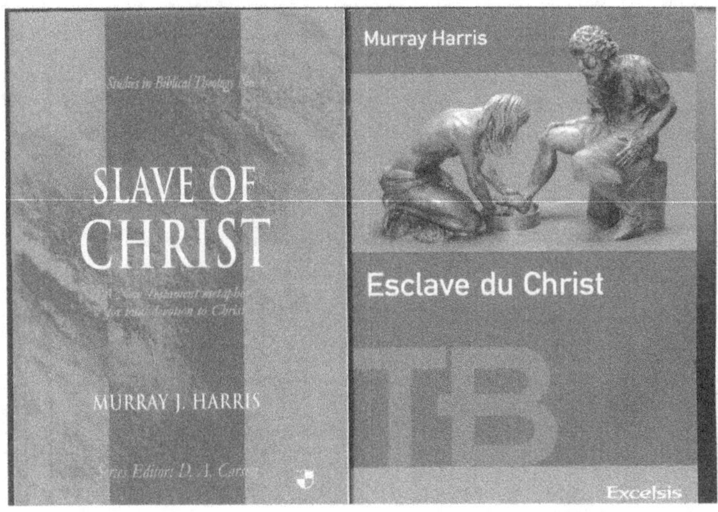

Illustration 10: Covers of *Slave of Christ* (1999 English, 2009 French)

1. French ed., *Esclave du Christ* (Charols, Fr.: Éditions Excelsis, 2009).

Churchman, Volume 113, Number 4, 1999

SLAVE OF CHRIST: A NEW TESTAMENT METAPHOR FOR TOTAL DEVOTION TO CHRIST
(New Studies in Biblical Theology No 8)   Murray J Harris
Leicester: Apollos 1999   224pp   £12.99   pb   ISBN 085111-517-9

This is a superb piece of evangelical scholarship. It is carefully thought out in method and execution, rigorously argued, comprehensively researched and highly stimulating. The author displays great skill in history, exegesis and theology, harnessing them all for the sake of a pastoral motive: to encourage greater devotion to Christ. It is an excellent example of how 'academic' study can feed and enliven preaching. The busy pastor-teacher with little time for reading beyond preparation for the next sermon, will undoubtedly find that for the long term, this book repays careful study.

Harris begins by noting that the word δοῦλός is the most distinctive Greek term for 'slave'. Yet it has consistently been translated by most modern versions as 'servant'. 'In twentieth century Christianity', he says, 'we have replaced the expression "total surrender" with the word "commitment", and "slave" with "servant".' This has important consequences for how we view our lives as Christians: 'we *commit* ourselves to *do* something, but when we surrender ourselves to someone [as slaves], we give ourselves up' (p 18). The rest of the book goes on to show how much of the New Testament's message is missed by mis-translating the Greek word. After a fascinating study of the differences between Greek, Roman and Jewish ideas of slavery he proceeds to an examination of the NT attitude to physical slavery. He shows that the NT accurately reflects the circumstances under which slavery operated in the first century and then considers the vexed question of why a full frontal assault was not made upon the institution of slavery itself. 'If Christianity is viewed as basically a movement of social reform, then this silence regarding slavery is indeed surprising, if not culpable' he says (p 67), and goes on to assert that Christianity is concerned primarily with the transformation of character and conduct rather than the reformation of societal structures.

However, the bulk of the book is concerned not with physical slavery but with the metaphor of slavery to Christ in the NT. There is some excellent exegesis here, and some nuggets of gold in the footnotes. Harris illuminates every verse he touches upon, unveiling their background in the culture of slavery. His discussion of the language of 'lordship' is especially enlightening (pp 87-105). There is some fairly dense argumentation at times, which may frustrate the casual reader. There are also some concise summaries of other scholarship (cf the interaction with Sass and Martin in ch 7) during which the reader becomes aware that the author has done a great deal of work in order to make the issues as clear as he can.

Harris is properly balanced in his exposition of the theme of slavery in the NT. At no point is he reductionistic about the metaphors the NT gives us, and he does not suggest that he has discovered a new 'centre' for the corpus. Indeed, he is honest about the fact that there are certain aspects of slavery which no longer apply in Christian experience (p 149; cf the two verses where Christians are 'no longer slaves' – John 15 and Galatians 4). In working through some NT examples of people commended as slaves of Christ he indulges in some speculation, but it is helpful to see these practical models of slavery worked out.

There are three exceedingly useful appendices (on the use of δοῦλός in the LXX, NT terms denoting slavery, and the translation of δοῦλός in the English versions) a nine page bibliography, an index of authors, subjects, Greek and Latin terms, biblical references and references to other ancient literature. This is a comprehensive work, a model piece of scholarship which shows us the workings as well as the conclusions, and a highly stimulating read. Buy it, read it, preach it!

LEE GATISS

Illustration 11: Review of *Slave of Christ*

I. GREEK TERMS DENOTING SLAVERY

The Greek language has an unparalleled range of words describing slavery. A famous passage in Philo illustrates this truth. As the writer amplifies the details of the Joseph saga, he describes the reaction of Joseph's brothers after the silver cup had been discovered in Benjamin's sack and they had returned to Egypt.

> They gave themselves up to him [Joseph] and volunteered to submit to slavery [*douleia*]. They called him their absolute master [*despotēs*] and spoke of themselves as foreign captives [*problētoi*], as slaves born and bred in the house [*oikotribes*], as slaves bought in the market [*argyrōnētoi*], omitting to mention no name indicative of slavery [*oiketika onomata*].[2]

The only terms derived from the *doul-* root that are used in the NT are as follows:

- *Doulos*, "slave" (male or female)

- *Doulē*, "female slave"

- *Syndoulos*, "fellow slave"

- *Douleia*, "slavery"

- *Doulos* (the cognate adjective), "subservient to," "in slavery to" (only in Rom 6:19, twice)

- *Douleuō*, "be a slave," "serve as a slave"

- *Douloō*, "enslave"

- *Katadouloō*, "reduce to slavery"

- *Doulagōgeō*, "take into slavery"

- *Ophthalmodoulia*, (lit.) "enslavement to the eye" ("eye-service")

---

2. Philo, *De Josepho* 219.

II. THE BIBLICAL USE OF THE GREEK TERM *DOULOS*

In the Septuagint (LXX)[3]

Roughly two-thirds of the LXX instances occur in the historical books (229 out of 378). Elsewhere the term is common only in the Psalms (55 instances), where it usually refers to the righteous Israelite who continues wholeheartedly in Yahweh's way (e.g., 3 Kgdms 8:23).

The main uses of *doulos* fall into two categories:

1. Any person or group in a temporary or permanent position of subservience to, or dependence on, or inferiority to another person or group—such as a menial worker, a king's soldiers or subjects, a prophet's suppliants, or a subservient nation

2. Individuals such as the patriarchs (e.g., Abraham, Ps 104:42), national leaders (David, Ps 88;4, 21), prophets (Elijah, 3 Kgdms 20:28), or anyone involved in the worship or service of God (Ps 133:1)

In the New Testament[4]

Figurative uses of the *doul-* root, with literal uses in brackets:

Book	*Doulos* (noun)	*Doulē*	*Syndou-los*	*Douleia*	*Douleuō*	*Douloō*
Whole NT	124x	3x	10x	5x	25x	8x
Matthew	1 (29)		(5)		1 (1)	
Mark	1 (4)					
Luke	1 (25)	2			2 (1)	

3. Harris, *Slave*, 173–75.

4. Harris, *Slave*, 177–79.

John	2 (9)				1	
Acts	3	1			1 (1)	(1)
Paul	16 (14)		2	4	15 (2)	6
Peter	1					1
Hebrews				1		
James	1					
Jude	1					
Revelation	11 (3)		3			
(The *doul-* root does not occur in the three Johannine epistles)						

Observations on these data:

1. In the four Gospels the literal use of *doulos* is (not surprisingly) normative, with the figurative use being exceptional (five cases).

2. In Paul's letters the literal and figurative uses of *doulos* (found side by side in 1 Cor 7:22) are almost evenly balanced.

3. Six of the metaphorical uses of *doulos* are found in epistolary salutations (Rom 1:1; Phil 1:1; Tit 1:1; Jas 1:1; 2 Pet 1:1; Jude 1; cf. Rev 1:1, twice).

4. When all the words drawn from the *doul-* stem are considered (180 in all—see the two lists above), 64 (that is, 36 percent) occur in the Pauline epistles.

5. The terms *doulos* and *diakonos* are closely associated. For instance, within one letter Paul calls his colleague Epaphras both "a loyal servant of Christ" (*pistos . . . diakonos tou Christou*, Col 1:7) and "a slave of Christ Jesus" (*doulos Christou Iēsou*, Col 4:12). A *doulos* gives service (*diakonia*), as is illustrated by the sequence *doulon . . . diakonei* in Luke 17:7–8. Yet not all those who give service are "slaves." The ruler who serves

by exercising authority and wielding the sword is called God's servant (*diakonos*), not his slave (Rom 13:3–4, 6). All "slaves" are "servants," but not all "servants" are "slaves"; *diakonos* is the broader term. Another important difference between the two words is that a *diakonos* may render his service under a negotiated contract as a wage earner, whereas **both the work *and* the person of a *doulos* belong wholly to another.**

III. THE METAPHOR OF SLAVERY

Slave imagery in the NT owes its origin to two sources: Greco-Roman society and ancient Near Eastern custom. Among ancient cultures, slavery as an institution essential to the production and lifestyle of a society was found only in classical Greece and classical Rome.[5] These societies were based on slavery. Since slavery still flourished in first-century AD Greco-Roman society, it is a priori likely that the NT motif of spiritual slavery should have one of its roots in the contemporary practice and language of physical slavery. As for the ancient Near East roots, E. Yamauchi has demonstrated that "one has great difficulty in finding a culture in the Near East that does *not* have the 'slave of God' motif" and concludes that "the practice of designating oneself as the Slave of one's God has been maintained for at least 4000 years to this day."[6]

However much we moderns, living on the other side of the abolition of formal slavery, may be scandalized by the NT use of the imagery of slavery to depict one aspect of our ideal relationship to the Deity, we cannot eradicate such imagery from the NT without compromising its message. Not only is there slavery to sin and lust, which is condemned, but slavery to God or Christ (see sect. IV below), which is encouraged. Moreover, God and his exalted Messiah are both given the titles *Kyrios* (Sovereign Lord; e.g., Rev 11:15, 17, of God; e.g., 1 Cor 8:6, of Christ) and *Despotēs* (Absolute Lord; e.g.,

5. Moses I. Finley, "A Peculiar Institution?," *Times Literary Supplement* (July 2, 1976) 819.

6. E. Yamauchi, "Slaves of God," *Bulletin of the Evangelical Theological Society* 9 (1966) 31, 35.

Luke 2:29; Acts 4:24; Rev 6:10, of God; 2 Pet 2:1; Jude 4, of Christ), terms that themselves imply absolute sovereignty over slaves. Nor should we overlook the fact that the final picture the NT gives of the eternal state is one where "slaves" (*douloi*) are completely devoted to the worship and service (*latreusousin*) of the Lord God and the Lamb (Rev 22:3). The redeemed remain "slaves" although their service is that of priests (cf. Rev 1:6; 5: 10; 20:6).

It is true that some slaves saw their situation as a means of upward social mobility, especially if their master was wealthy and influential. But in the view of free citizens, the slave represented "the scum of the earth" (1 Cor 4:13), however elevated his role in the slave owner's household and however famous his master. Only when a slave had become a freedman, had attained Roman citizenship, and had entered a client-patron relationship with his former master would the status of an ex-slave become significant in the eyes of free persons. And even then a freedman's background was not forgotten.

But the NT eradicated the negative connotations that attached to the notion of slavery when it described the Christian's slavery to Christ or God. As used of the believer's exclusive devotion to the Lord Christ, the term *doulos* is not partially sweet and partially sour but totally sweet. The Paul who called himself "a slave of Christ Jesus" (Rom 1:1) and spoke of all Christians, whether slave or free, as the slaves of Christ (1 Cor 7:22; Eph 6:6) affirms that believers have not received "the spirit of slavery" (*pneuma douleias*) or "the spirit of a slave" that would prompt a return to fear (Rom 8:15). Cringing servility or abject submission to a master, born of fear, has no place in the Christian's slavery to Christ.

This willing servitude to the risen Christ includes three elements:

1. Humble submission to the person of Christ. This involves an acknowledgment that, as supreme Lord, he has absolute and exclusive rights to the will, affections, and energy, now and forever.

2. Unquestioning obedience to the Master's will

3. An exclusive preoccupation with pleasing Christ. "We make it our ambition," says Paul, "to be constantly pleasing to him" (2 Cor 5:9). This was Paul's magnificent obsession, an obsession that had the effect of expelling inferior—albeit legitimate—pursuits.

All metaphors have limitations. In the two places where we are told that Christians are "no longer" slaves (John 15:15; Gal 4:7), we may deduce from the context the aspects of slavery that do not apply to Christian experience.

1. A slave did not have an intimate acquaintance with his master's thoughts and plans; a master did not count his slaves as his friends (cf. John 15:14–15).

2. A slave did not expect to be adopted into his master's family or to receive an inheritance (cf. Gal 4:1–7).

But as matters now stand, the followers of Jesus, unlike the slave, have gained an intimate knowledge of the Master (John 10:14; Eph 1:17; Phil 3:10), have been adopted into the Master's family (Gal 4:5), and will receive the Master's inheritance (Rom 8:17).

IV. "SLAVE OF GOD" AND "SLAVE OF CHRIST"

The NT data about these two concepts are as follows.

a. The expression "**slave(s) of God**"
In the plural (*douloi theou*): Acts 2:18; 4:29; 16:17; 1 Pet 2:16; Rev 1:1a; 7:3; 10:7; 11:8; 19:2, 5; 22:3, 6

In the singular (*doulos theou*): Luke 1:38, 48; 2:29; Titus 1:1; Jas 1:1; Rev 1:1b; 15:3

b. The expression "**slave(s) of Christ**"
In the plural (*douloi Christou*): Eph 6:6; Phil 1:1; Rev 2:20

In the singular (*doulos Christou*): Rom 1:1; Gal 1:10; 1 Cor
7:22; Col 4:12; 2 Tim 2:24; Jas 1:1; 2 Pet 1:1;
Jude 1

Clearly Christians do not have two competing Masters, each vying for total allegiance. Just as the Spirit of Christ is none other than the Spirit of God (Rom 8:9), so also, to give a slave's service to Christ is indistinguishable from giving such service to God—so James could introduce himself as "a slave of God and of the Lord Jesus Christ" (Jas 1:1).

It is remarkable that both of the leading figures in the early church chose to introduce themselves as a "slave" (*doulos*) and "apostle" of the risen Christ—"Paul, a slave of Christ Jesus, called to be an apostle" (Rom 1:1) and "Simon Peter, a slave and apostle of Jesus Christ" (2 Pet 1:1). Does not the order "slave—apostle" suggest that both Paul and Peter regarded their slavery to Christ to be even more important than their being his apostles?

V. THE TRANSLATION OF *DOULOS* IN EVV

A. A Strange Phenomenon

In NT Greek there are at least six terms that are often translated or could be translated by the English word "servant" (viz. *diakonos, oiketēs, pais, hypēretēs, leitourgos, paidiskē*). But only one NT word—*doulos* (or the cognate noun *doulē*, "female slave")—has the distinctive meaning of "slave," and this word occurs 124 times in the NT and its compound form *syndoulos* (fellow slave) 10 times.

Yet in the history of the English Bible we find the strange but common tradition of generally avoiding the rendering "slave" for *doulos*, unless literal slavery or slavery to something inanimate is in mind—as in the "slave-free" antithesis, in the household codes of conduct, or in reference to slavery to sin. A potent illustration of this remarkable fact and the dilemma faced by translators is afforded by Eph 6:5–6, where, in a single Greek sentence, there are two instances of *douloi* (plural), one literal (*douloi* who have "earthly masters," v. 5), and one figurative (*douloi* of Christ, v. 6). Most EVV, rightly I believe, have:

- "slaves . . . slaves" (TCNT, NEB, REB, JB, NJB, NASB, GNB, HCSB, NASB, NAB1, NIV, CEV, NRSV, NLT, LSB, Goodspeed [who elsewhere almost always renders *doulos* by "slave"])

But others have:

- "servants . . . servants" (KJV, RV, Moffatt)
- "slaves . . . servants" (RSV, Phillips, Cassirer)
- "slaves . . . bondservants" (Weymouth")
- "bondservants . . . bondservants" (NJKV, ESV)

The ESV preface says, "The ESV translates the word [*doulos*] as 'slave' when someone had little hope of becoming free. It translates the word as 'bondservant' when someone could gain freedom by paying a set price or by serving for a set length of time. It translates the word 'servant' when a person simply worked for someone else."[7] It is difficult to see how believers are "bondservants of Christ" in this sense.

B. Reasons for This Phenomenon

1. Painful historical memories in the UK and the US regarding slavery. Why perpetuate those disconcerting memories by enshrining in Holy Scripture an institution that has always deserved to be abhorred? But we should not overlook the fact that throughout the first-century Roman Empire there was (it is estimated) one slave for every five free persons, so that, for example, the infant house church in Roman Corinth might have included six or seven slaves (which may explain 1 Cor 11:21–22).

7. ESV, x.

2. Some translators are reticent to use the term "slave" out of fear that their readers may project their secondhand knowledge of modern slavery back into the first century, when slavery had a considerably different complexion.

In the first century, slaves were not distinguishable from free persons by race, speech, or clothing; they were sometimes more highly educated than their masters and held responsible professional positions; some people sold themselves into slavery for economic or social advantage; they could reasonably hope to be emancipated after ten to twenty years of service or by their thirties at the latest; they were not denied the right of public assembly and were not socially segregated (at least in the cities); they could accumulate savings to buy their freedom; their natural inferiority was not assumed.

These differences between ancient and modern slavery are not grounds for purging the language of slavery from the NT but rather for its preservation, given the ubiquity of slavery in the first century as the substratum of society. That is, if the language of slavery is offensive, the offence would have been considerably greater for those who lived in societies where slavery was intrinsic rather than for us for whom slavery is simply an unpleasant and embarrassing memory.

There are some linguistic facts that may in part explain the preference for "servant" over "slave":

- "In the 14th and 15th c[enturies] [*servant* was] often used to render the L[atin] *servus* slave. In all the Bible translations from Wyclif to the Revised Version of 1880–84, the word very often represents the Heb. *ebed* or the Gk. *doulos*, which correspond to *slave*, though this term as applied to Israelitish conditions would perh[aps] be misleading."[8]

- The KJV avoided the term "slave" (except for Jer 2:14; Rev 18:13), perhaps because in Elizabethan English it denoted a captive in fetters or a prisoner in jail. In this way and in a

8. *OED*, 9:508, 3.a.

multitude of other cases, the KJV has exercised a formative influence on subsequent translations.

- "In the North American colonies in the 17–18th c[enturies], and subsequently in the United States, *servant* was the usual designation for a slave."[9]

C. The Present Situation Regarding "Servant" and "Slave" in Translation

In modern English, the terms "servant" and "slave" share some common conceptual territory, for they may both refer to a person who renders service to someone else. But whereas a slave belongs to another person as a chattel and does not have the right to discontinue service, a servant may be in the employ of another person as a wage earner. Every slave is a servant in that he or she is obliged to do the bidding of a superior, but not every servant is a slave, for they could be discharged or may choose to resign. My definition of a slave is "someone whose person and service belong wholly to another." What better description of "the slave of Christ"?

The strongest support for rendering *doulos* by "slave" comes from lexicographers, who, while not translators, are not unaware of the need for sensitivity to the dominant connotations of a word on the "receptor language." The three most distinguished NT lexicographers of recent times are G. A. Deissmann, Walter Bauer, and Ceslas Spicq. Deissmann comments that "the translation of *doulos* by 'servant' rather than 'slave' [led] to the total effacement of its ancient significance."[10] BDAG, essentially the pioneering work of Bauer, proposes "slave" as the appropriate rendering of *doulos* everywhere in the NT except for the few places where a

9. *OED*, 9:508, 3.b.

10. Adolf Deissman, *Light from the Ancient East: The New Testament Illustrated by Recently Discovered Texts of the Graeco-Roman World*, translated by Lionel R. M. Strachan (Grand Rapids: Baker, 1965; English translation of 1922 German ed.), 319.

king's officials are "ministers."[11] Finally, Spicq begins his treatment of *doulos* with the blunt affirmation, "It is wrong to translate *doulos* as 'servant,' so obscuring its precise signification in the language of the first century."[12] Similar sentiments are expressed by S. S. Bartchy, an authority on first-century slavery: "In contrast to the Authorised Version's translation of the Gk term *doulos* as 'servant,' the word 'slave' should be used in order to stress the legally regulated subordination of the person in slavery. Yet in contrast to present connotations of the term 'slave' resulting from the specific racial, economic, educational, and political practices characteristic of slavery in the New World, the slaves and slavery mentioned in NT texts must be defined strictly in terms of the profoundly different legal-social contexts of the 1st century C. E."[13]

Translators should continue to use "slave" for *doulos* (1) in the "slave-free" antithesis; (2) in the "household tables," where masters and slaves are mentioned; and (3) when slavery is to something impersonal (such as sin, depravity, or obedience). But the area where translators need to be more courageous is in translating the term *doulos* as "slave" in reference to the Christian's relation to Christ or God

I believe a breakthrough will occur for any modern English translation when it renders *doulos* by "slave" in Rom 1:1 and Phil 2:7: "Paul, a slave of Christ Jesus" and "[Christ Jesus] emptied himself by taking the form of a slave."[14]

11. BDAG, 260 a–c.

12. Ceslas Spicq, *Theological Lexicon of the New Testament* (Peabody, MA: Hendrickson, 1994), 1:380.

13. S. S. Bartchy, "Slavery: New Testament," in *The Anchor Bible Dictionary*, edited by D. N. Freedman (New York: Doubleday, 1992), 6:66.

14. Similarly NAB2, NLT, NRSV (footnote in Rom 1:1), LSB, Goodspeed.

Chapter 8

Final Observations

1. No one can deny the distinctive role that the NIV has played in the history of the Bible in English. From 1611 until the mid-1980s the KJV reigned supreme among English readers of the Bible until it yielded its supremacy to the NIV. Not surprisingly, the same vigorous opposition that greeted the arrival of the KJV in 1611 was also meted out to the NIV when it appeared in 1978. "How dare you try to replace the authorised Bishops' Bible!" became "How dare you touch my King James Version!" But in each case the hostility was finally stifled by the sheer beauty of the new arrival.

The dominance of the NIV was soon challenged by the appearance of newly updated alternatives such as the NRSV (1989) and REB (1990), not to speak of the existing alternatives such as the TEV (1966), JB (1966), NAB1 (1970), GNB (1976), NASB (1977), and now the relatively recent versions such as the NJB (1985), NCV (1987), GNT (1992), CEV (1995), NLT (1996), HCSB (2001), and ESV (2001).

In spite of this fierce competition for the English Bible market, the NIV has managed to maintain its supremacy, with over five hundred million copies sold worldwide and millions more distributed free of charge by the New York Bible Society (now Biblica). What accounts for this continuing popularity? In a nutshell, it is the NIV's delicate blend of attractive readability and traditional cadences, along with its source in evangelical scholars who represent a wide variety of Christian denominations.

2. The TNIV (Today's NIV) of 2001 and 2005 came under heavy attack for its gentle foray into "gender-neutral" territory. As a consequence, all inclusive language changes in the TNIV were reconsidered in preparation for the 2011 edition. Some of those changes were retained, some were rejected in favor of the 1984 rendering, while many were restated in an alternative way.[1]

The majority of modern versions now incorporate some accommodation to the undeniable contemporary changes in gender terminology. In these versions it is now common to read "the person who . . . they/them/their" in place of "he who . . . he/him/his." Examples of this pleasing trend is the willingness to render *adelphoi* (brothers) by "brothers and sisters," as seen in the changes in this direction from the HCSB of 2001 to the CSB of 2017, and from the 1977 edition of the NASB to its 2020 edition.[2]

3. In ch. 7 I discussed "A Perennial Translation Problem"—how to translate the Greek word *doulos* appropriately—and suggested that translators should be more courageous in rendering the word by "slave" in describing the relationship of the believer to Christ and God. I trust the present trend to do this, as in NAB2, NLT, LSB, and Goodspeed, will continue and accelerate, for a crucial aspect of Christian experience is at stake.

Dr. John MacArthur of Grace Community Church in Sun Valley, California, is a well-known, influential, and controversial

1. See further on this issue the comprehensive CBT report of August 2010, "Updating the New International Version of the Bible: Notes from the Committee on Bible Translation," 4–7 (https://s35422.pcdn.co/wp-content/uploads/2014/11/2011-Translation-Notes.pdf).

2. As observed by Mark Strauss, "The World's Most Popular Bible: A History of the New International Version (NIV)" (https://www.logos.com/grow/min-history-of-the-niv-bible/).

figure on the Christian landscape. In the preface to his book *Slave: The Hidden Truth about Your Identity in Christ*, he relates that it was during an all-night flight to London in the spring of 2007 that he read a book entitled *Slave of Christ* by a certain Murray J. Harris. The topic prompted him to recognize a monumental gap in his thinking. "After more than fifty years of translating, studying, teaching, preaching, and writing through the New Testament, I thought I had its truths pretty well identified and understood—especially on the realm of the New Testament theology of the gospel."[3] But now he had unexpectedly discovered a hidden gem in NT thought. I confess I disagree with MacArthur's assertion that there has been a "cover-up" by English NT translators of this truth about the Christian's "slavery" to Christ or God, but I agree with him that this emancipating reality has been long overlooked. He comments, "As I began to dig down into this buried jewel of the gospel, its pervasive splendor began to dominate my thinking and preaching. Every time and everywhere I addressed the subject, the response was the same—startled wonder."[4]

I frequently describe Paul's letter to the Romans as the flagship of the Pauline fleet. To develop the metaphor, flying proudly at the top of the mast of this ship is a flag bearing the words "Paul, a slave of Christ Jesus" (*Paulos, doulos Christou Iēsou*, Rom 1:1a). This flag is two-toned, its white indicating complete freedom yet total surrender, and its purple symbolizing royal ownership and therefore incomparable privilege. The *doulos* concept signifies all four of these features when it describes the Christian's relationship to God and Christ.

Is it not significant that four letters of the New Testament—by Paul, Peter, Jude, and James—all begin with the author's claim to be a *doulos* of Christ (Rom 1:1; 2 Pet 1:1; Jude 1; Jas 1:1)? Hopefully, this neglected facet of NT theology will regain the place it deserves.

3. John MacArthur, *Slave: The Truth about Your Hidden Identity in Christ* (Nashville: Thomas Nelson, 2010), 1.

4. MacArthur, *Slave*, 2.